GREAT MOMENTS

IN SOUTH AFRICAN SPORT

Paul Dobson

DON NELSON
CAPE TOWN

First Edition 1988

ISBN 1 86806 054 3

Cover photographs: Cape Times and Anne Laing

Cover designed by Poul-Ejnar Hansen

Photo-typesetting and Reproduction by Unifoto
Printed by CTP Book Printers

South African sport has produced many moments of heart-stopping excitement and its impact on the international scene was, until politics barred us from competing overseas, always one which commanded great respect.

This book relates 23 of those great moments, stories which in some cases have been handed down from father to son and others which are still discussed in sporting clubs and at dinner parties.

Paul Dobson has researched extensively and cleverly interwoven words from books now out of print written by some of our greatest sportswriters.

Contents

Paul Dobson has, on his own admission, always been a sports fanatic though rugby has always enjoyed preference and it is in this sport that he made his mark as a referee at provincial level. He also serves on the executive of the W.P. Referees' Society, the W.P. High Schools' Union, the W.P. Rugby Bureau and is a member of the S.A. Rugby Board's coaching structure and Publications Committee.

He has written extensively for sports publications.

He was born in Cape Town, went to school at St. Joseph's College and studied in Australia and Pietermaritzburg before he began teaching in Natal in 1958. He is at present teaching at Diocesan College where he has been since 1966. He is married with three children.

For all those who,
starting with my parents,
have taught me to love sport
and for all those,
especially Margaret and the children,
who help me to write about it.

Foreword

This is a sample of great moments in South African sport. Of course, people will disagree with the choice and, of course, others could have been made. It is a sample. It also contains samples of great writing on sport in South Africa, especially from eye-witness accounts. No attempt has been made to hide such writings and only honour is intended by their inclusion.

There is much to glory in and also much cause for sadness and nostalgia. Those good old days when South Africans were honourable combatants on the world's playing fields are no more.

Opportunity will return, and then above all the memory of what has happened will be important, as we shall need the traditions of the past to build proud performances in the future. Our day will come again.

A TASTE OF SUCCESS

ricket can be dull, but no sport can cause the exquisite
rture of excitement which cricket can when it builds to a
imax. The match will take its course day after day and then
e picture is suddenly clear. All the options are starkly
bvious, and a single mistake can be decisive.

One ball can cause agony or ecstasy, depending on your
oint of view. Matches which produce this sort of thrill stay
rever in the memory and in the history of the game. At the
ry beginning of 1906 there was one such at the Wanderers
the Old Wanderers, that is – which is still a record of its sort
the history of test cricket as played throughout the world.

By that time South Africa had suffered ten defeats, most
f them thrashings, without a victory in test cricket. On the
904 tour to England it had not even been granted a test
atch though the South Africans did remarkably well once
ey made the transition from matting to turf.

In 1906 they would play five tests against England when
elham 'Plum' Warner brought the MCC. From then on
outh Africa would play tests – that is till politicians conspired
cut them down in the full bloom of their ability.

Plum Warner, later president of the MCC and Sir Pelham,
rought a strong side though he did note that it was hard for
mateurs to get away for a five-month tour, and four turned
own the invitation – that dashing batsman RH Spooner,
who, in Neville Cardus's words, "put a bloom on the un-
rthodox" and who would later turn down the captaincy of
England on a tour to Australia, Spooner who had been in
South Africa for the Anglo-Boer War; JR Mason, the Kent
aptain, who had retired; H Martyn of Somerset, a splendid
itter and an almost incomparable wicket-keeper; and, above
ll, BFT Bosanquet, who had taken 9/107 against the South
Africans at Lord's in the very first match of the 1904 tour

and whose "presence" was so significant in the affairs South Africa at the beginning of 1906.

Plum Warner had what he calls a 'good sound team, ar one that appeared strong enough for the purpose'. And tl tour went according to plan. They trounced Western Provi and Griquas twice each besides handing out thrashings concoctions of minnows, one with 18 players, the other wi 15.

Then they came to Johannesburg to meet Transva followed by an excursion to pretty Potchefstroom to gre the local Britishers before the serious business of the first te: But a shock occurred. As Ali Bacher's side did to Bobt Simpson's Australians sixty years later, so Percy Sherwell Transvaal team showed that a touring team could be beate

Oh, it all looked innocent enough at first when the MC bundled Transvaal out for 135 and then scored 265 then selves. Transvaal fared better when everybody got runs in tl second innings and they scored 305, leaving the MCC 176 t win. That did not look a problem, but they did not get then Reggie Schwartz took 5/34, Aubrey Faulkner 3/62 and Jimm Sinclair 2/11. The *Cape Times* report of the match cal dismissing the mighty MCC for such a meagre total "one the finest cricketting feats achieved in this or any othe country". It also revealed the "glorious uncertainty of cricket

What was most significant was that two Transvaler: Schwartz and Faulkner, were bowling googlies or Bosies a they were often called from their inventor. Schwartz ha picked it up. He had been at Oxford with Bosanquet befor accepting the post of Abe Bailey's secretary and migrating t South Africa.

In 1903 Bosanquet invented the googly and in 190 Schwartz met up with him, no longer as an Oxford an Middlesex team mate, but as a touring South African, an his old university chum let him into the secret. Schwart brought it back to South Africa where it was expeciall suited to the matting wickets which were to be found every where from the Cape to the Zambezi.

Much of South Africa's cricketing success is due to th crop of googly bowlers whom Schwartz taught – Faulkner

Ernie Vogler of the Eastern Province who was the first man to take 10 wickets in an innings in a Currie Cup match (The second was Stephen Jeffreys in 1986), and Gordon White, more famous as a batsman.

Warner says this of the matting wickets, "Finger-spin bowlers like Schwartz, Faulkner, and Vogler were suited exactly by the matting wickets on which it is so difficult to jump out and drive, and on which the ball not only turns twice as much and twice as quickly as on grass, but occasionally gets up a little. Over and over again Vogler would pitch an inch or two outside the leg-stump and miss the off by a foot while Schwartz could do even more the other way. On two occasions he bowled me balls which pitched six or seven inches wide of the off-stump, and then, just touching the outside of my left pad as I stepped across, hit the leg-stump."

The MCC took the defeat hard as they went off to picnic in Potchefstroom. There was even talk that they had cabled for prominent players from England, a rumour which The *Cape Times* correspondent thought especially malicious.

The South African team selected to play England starting on New Year's Day at the Wanderers had eight Transvalers with Sibley Snooke from Western Province, Ernie Vogler from Eastern Province, and Dave Nourse from Natal.

The Transvalers were Louis Tancred, Maitland Hathorn, Gordon White, Jimmy Sinclair, Aubrey Faulkner, Reggie Schwartz, Bill Shalders, and the captain and wicket-keeper, Percy Sherwell, the South African men's tennis champion. Nourse was born in Croyden and came out as a soldier and Schwartz was from Kent. The rest were South African born.

These eleven players played in all five of the tests, and that has not happened since in South African cricket history.

Plum Warner won the toss and England batted first on the red dust of the Wanderers with its strip of matting. And soon they were in trouble– 15/3 to South Africa's opening attack, an attack very different from great pairs of openers in the future like Adcock and Heine, and Pollock and Proctor. The openers were Schwartz and Faulkner, and they both bowled googlies!

The MCC recovered. Schofield Haigh was dropped and

young Jack Crawford batted really well for 44. The tail wagged, Colin Blythe getting 17 at number 11. England made 184. Not great, but marvellous by the standard of the South African's performance in the first innings as Walter Lees, Colin Blythe and Jack Crawford sent them scampering back for 91. It could have been even worse but down at the tail of the South African innings Dave Nourse, Tip Snooke and Ernie Vogler got into double figures.

That, too, was not surprising as the South African team of 1906 was blessed with allrounders not to be repeated in South African cricket for another sixty years. Percy Sherwell, the wicket-keeper, was at number 11. He opened the batting for South Africa at Lord's and scored the first South African test century at that great ground in 1907– a century in only 95 minutes, the second fastest test century in South African test history.

Schwartz at number 10 had scored a century at Lord's against an England X1 and was worth his place in the side as a batsman alone. Ernie Vogler at number 9 hit 62 in a last wicket stand of 94 with Sherwell in the fifth test, a partnership which lasted an hour and a quarter. Vogler was not out at the end and the crowd was so delighted that they subscribed £47 13s 9d for him.

As Warner said, "Nearly every eleven has a "rabbit" or two at the end; but the South African X1 was like the Manx cat – it had no tail." Those words are worth remembering in the light of what was to happen at the Wanderers.

In the England second innings Plum Warner got a half-century but their end result was much as in the first – 190 all out. Schwartz, Vogler and Faulkner got eight amongst them with their googlies. South Africa had to make 284 to win. Who would bet on them?

At close of play on the second day the South Africans were 68/2. Colin Blythe, the left arm spinner who opened the bowling with Walter Lees had Louis Tancred caught by Warner for 10 and Maitland Hathorn, one of South Africa's batting hopes, was out for 4.

There was excitement at the start of the third and final day. His Excellency Lord Selborne was down at the Wanderers early to secure a place of vantage under the trees, and there were 800 spectators at the start. That number would grow during the day.

Shalders and White were to continue for South Africa, Shalders on 38. Lees opened the attack, and, oddly, as he had bowled the last over the night before, he was allowed by by the laws of the day to bowl the first over the following day, two overs in succession. He bowled from the Hospital end while Colin Blythe operated from the Railway end. The England attack was blunted by the absence of Schofield Haigh who had dysentery. His place in the field was taken by HDG Levenson-Gower (pronounced Lewson-Gorr) who captained the MCC team to South Africa in 1910 when the South Africans won the series.

Lees bowled a maiden. Blythe bowled a maiden. Lees bowled to Shalders who played it to Warner, who misfielded. Shalders called for a run, which White declined. Shalders turned. Crawford who had covered Warner, gathered, returned, hit the wicket, and ran Shalders out. 68 for 3, last man 38. Silbey Snooke joined White, and runs came slowly but Snooke seemed to be settling in when Lees trapped him leg before. 82-4-9. It was a long way to go.

In came Jimmy Sinclair, the man who hit a century in 80 minutes in a test against Joe Darling's Australians, a man described as "all wire and whipcord". Sinclair would not potter. He took a single off Blythe and smashed Lees for a four. But he was a man who could not restrain himself. He lofted Lees down to long-on where Fane held a good catch. 89-5-5, with Gordon White on 23.

Aubrey Faulkner was next at bat. After Trevor Goddard he remains South Africa's most successful allrounder though when he had played in the Western Province shortly before that he was considered "a very moderate cricketer, scarcely up to club form". Runs were being eked out. At 99 Warner brought on Crawford for Blythe, and a leg-bye off White saw the 100 up in $2\frac{1}{4}$ hours. That was regarded as remarkably slow batting. There have been many slower performances since!

Disaster was not slow coming. White snicked one down on

the leg side and the batsmen set off. So did Board, the wicket-keeper. He scampered after the ball, got it and was almost prone when he threw it back. It hit the stumps. Faulkner was run out. The swelling crowd groaned, plunged into despair. 105-6-6.

Cometh the hour, cometh the man. The man was Dave Nourse, a bowler who batted more than he bowled in the series. Alfred Relf gave Lees a rest at the Hospital end but the runs kept coming. Nourse prodded and turned it around on the leg side, while White played it as straight as could be. Nourse hit Crawford to the boundary to bring up 120. There were still 164 runs needed. Nourse took two more fours and when the players went in to lunch the score was 134/6 with White on 36 and Nourse on 23. 150 runs needed.

The Old Wanderers, situated in the centre of Johannesburg, was convenient. The news went round the offices and business houses. After lunch there were two thousand people in the ground and there was a steady stream of excited people bobbing in throughout the rest of the afternoon.

Blythe, Lees, and Relf shared the afternoon's bowling without much success, and the 150 came up. There were loud cheers when White cut Lees for four to bring up his half century in $3\frac{1}{4}$ hours.

Warner was getting desperate. First he brought Crawford back, and then he threw the ball to Wynyard who bowled "lobs". He puzzled White at first but gradually the two batsmen got on top of him. 170 came up. 114 to go. Nourse took two fours off Lees amid loud applause. 180 up, 104 to go. Nourse took a three off Blythe to go to 50. 190, 94 to go.

After four hours' batting South Africa had 200 on the board and the crowd were bubbling. Warner tried Hayes but the runs kept coming and the crowd was now cheering each run enthusiastically.

Cricket in the flick of a ball can drop you from euphoria deep into the slough of despair. Relf got one on a perfect length through White's normally impenetrable guard. The ball nicked the top of the bails. 225-7-81.

White had made 81 in 4 hours 10 minutes with 11 fours. The *Cape Times* report said, "It was the finest innings played against the team up to the present, being a great innings, a superb display of sound defensive cricket, varied by clean good strokes all round the wicket. He never gave a semblance of a chance." Plum Warner says, "He never looked like getting out; and it was his superb defence and judgement that helped to wear down our bowling."

In 2¼ hours White and Nourse had added 121 runs. Defensive cricket in those days obviously did not mean what it means today! It had in fact been a marvellous two hours – heroic batting, splendid bowling and what Percy Sherwell called "the most accurate and often brilliant fielding".

Ernie Vogler came out to bat. By now nerves were in tatters, earlier hopes uncertain. There were still 58 runs to get. There was quiet after White had been cheered into the pavilion.

Despair deepened. Five runs later Hayes bowled Vogler for 2. 230-8-2. Vogler could have hit the South Africans to quick victory, but no . . . .There were still 54 runs wanted. Out to bat came Reggie Schwartz to join big Dave Nourse and the pair went to tea with the score 236/8, Nourse on 71, Schwartz on 1.

Tea is often a good wicket taker. When the batsmen came out after tea, there were more than ten thousand hopefuls in the Wanderers, but their hopes looked on a slippery slide. And yet if you were a South African supporter in those days even this effort against the masters from "Home", was tantamount to victory.

The light was bad, rain was threatening, and Hayes continued from the Hospital end with Relf operating from the Railway end. Relf got one to kick. Schwartz prodded tamely and the bowler took a gentle return catch. 239-9-2.

There were 10 000 silent spectators in the ground, as Percy Sherwell, the skipper, came out to join Dave Nourse who appeared to have nerves of steel. It was Percy Sherwell's first test and he was the captain and the situation was nerve-racking. There were 45 runs to get.

There are different reactions to nerves. Some people freeze; those with the big match temperament come into their own. Percy Sherwell played cricket as he knew best– aggressively.

15

The fielders came crowding round the South African captain. He blocked two from Relf and let the third go through to the wicket-keeper. Then Relf tried to slower one. He overpitched and Sherwell drove him to the midwicket boundary. The silence burst in a relieved roar. Plum Warner lamented.

Four byes saw the 250 come up. Nourse snicked Lees to leg and moved to 82, the highest score of the match. The Nourse and Sherwell took turns to drive Lees for four, and the South Africans had 270 runs. The crowd in their hysteria alternated between wild outbursts and equally sudden silences.

On 273 Nourse got a streaky single on the leg side and the South Africans needed ten. Sherwell went to cut, got an edge and the ball skidded between the slips, who left it each to the other though it would have been a wonderful catch for either. And the ball kept on going– to the boundary for four. And the crowd cheered.

Four runs required for victory. Relf starts an over to Nourse and the left-hander nudges the first ball down to fine leg. Sherwell is off sprinting and he squeezes three runs out of the shot. The scores are tied. The crowd jumps and cheers and hats go flying into the air. "We cannot lose now," they shout.

When the uproar subsided, play resumed. The second ball of the over is outside the offstump and Sherwell lets it through to Board. The third is closer and Sherwell cuts. Slip fumbles, the batsmen think of the winning single, decide against it and stay their ground. The fourth ball Sherwell plays gently back along the ground to Relf, and even that humble stroke merits cheering. Relf drops the fifth ball short and Sherwell leaps at it. He drives and in a twinkling it is through the field and heading for the boundary.

South Africa has won!

The crowd streamed onto the field and the cricketers had difficulty reaching the pavilion. Plum Warner recalls, "Never have I witnessed anything like the scene at the finish. Men where shrieking hysterically, some were even crying, and hats and sticks were flying everywhere. When the winning hit had been made the crowd simply flung themselves at Nourse and

Sherwell and carried them into the pavilion, while, for half an hour after it was all over, thousands lingered on, and the whole of the South African team had to come forward on to the balcony of the committee room."

Abe Bailey, who had done so much for South African cricket, asked Warner to address the crowd, which he did, telling them, "In all my experience of cricket I have never seen a side fight a better rearguard action, and though beaten, and naturally the first person to regret the result, I was also the first person to appreciate the magnificent and splendid qualities which brought victory to your side." Those qualities, chauvinist that Warner was, he would see as "that grit and courage which we are proud of saying are inherent in the British race."

Leveson-Gower described it prophetically as a match that would "live long in the memory of those fortunate enough to watch it." Warner prophesied with even greater determination. "Defeat in such a struggle was glorious, for the first test will be talked of in South Africa as long as cricket is played there."

Scorecard: I have recorded it as Warner noted it. Amateurs (gentlemen) have initials, professionals (players) do not. Those were the days when players carried gentlemen's bags, when there were separate dressingrooms and entrances, when, on the MCC's visit to the army in Pretoria, the gentlemen were entertained in the officers' mess, the players in the sergeants'.

England: 1st Innings:

P.F. Warner c Snooke, b. Schwartz	6
F.L. Fane c. Schwartz, b. Faulkner	1
Denton c. Faulkner, b. Schwartz	0
Capt. E.G. Wynyard st. Sherwell, b. Schwartz	29
Hayes c. & b. Vogler	20
J.N. Crawford c. Nourse, b. Sinclair	44
Relf b. White	8
Haigh b. Faulkner	23
Board not out	9
Lees st. Sherwell, b. White	11

Blythe b. Sinclair   17
Extras   16
                    Total   184

Bowling:	O	M	R	W
Schwartz	21	5	72	3
Faulkner	22	7	35	2
Sinclair	11	1	36	2
Vogler	3	-	10	1
White	5	1	13	2
Nourse	1	-	2	0

South Africa: 1st Innings:
L.J. Tancred c. Board, b. Lees   3
W.A. Shalders c. Haigh, b. Blythe   4
M Hathorn b. Lees   5
J.H. Sinclair c. & b. Lees   0
G.A. Faulkner b. Blythe   4
G. White c. Blythe, b. Lees   8
S.J. Snooke c. Board, b. Blythe   19
A.W. Nourse not out   18
A.E. Vogler b. Crawford   14
R.O. Schwartz c. Relf, b. Crawford   5
P.W. Sherwell l.b.w., b. Lees   1
Extras   10
                    Total   91

Bowling:	O	M	R	W
Lees	23.1	10	34	5
Blythe	16	5	33	3
Crawford	7	1	14	2

England: 2nd Innings:
P.F. Warner b. Vogler   51
F.L. Fane b. Snooke   3
Denton b. Faulkner   34
Capt. E.G. Wynyard b. Vogler   0
Hayes c. Schwartz, b. Snooke   3
J.N. Crawford b. Nourse   43

Relf c. Sherwell, b. Faulkner				17
Haigh l.b.w., b. Nourse				0
Board l.b.w., b. Faulkner				7
Lees not out				1
Blythe b. Faulkner				0
Extras				31
Total				190

Bowling:	O	M	R	W
Snooke	12	4	38	2
Schwartz	8	1	24	0
Vogler	11	3	24	2
Faulkner	12.5	5	26	4
Sinclair	5	1	25	0
White	4	-	15	0
Nourse	6	4	7	2

South Africa: 2nd Innings:

L.J. Tancred c. Warner, b. Blythe				10
W.A. Shalders run out				38
M. Hathorn c. Crawford, b. Lees				4
J.H. Sinclair c. Fane, b. Lees				5
G White b. Relf				81
S.J. Snooke l.b.w., b. Lees				9
A.W. Nourse not out				93
A.E. Vogler b. Hayes				2
R.O. Schwartz c. & b. Relf				2
P.W. Sherwell not out				22
Extras				15
Total				287 (for 9 wkts)

Bowling:	O	M	R	W
Lees	33	10	74	3
Blythe	28	12	50	1
Crawford	17	4	49	0
Haigh	1	-	9	0
Relf	21.5	7	47	2
Wynyard	3	-	15	0
Hayes	9	-	28	1

"And so ended a match which deserves to rank amongst the classic contests of cricket, and one which I shall remember to my dying day," wrotes Warner.

The teams had a Smoking Concert that evening, attended amongst others by Abe Bailey and the Mayor of Johannesburg, Councillor JW Quinn. There were all kinds of jollities and some speeches. The mayor made one, longish, in which he referred to "a great triumph for the Transvaal, or rather for South Africa, which is the same thing", and after which he presented Dave Nourse with a cheque for £86-8s-3d, which the spectators had subscribed.

Dave Nourse's speech was brief. "Mr. Mayor, I am not much of a speech-maker, but I thank you one and all. Good night."

For South African cricket it was a beginning of many great things, the beginning of winning. They won that series 4-1, losing only at Newlands.

Six tests in world cricket history have been won by 1 wicket, but the partnership between Nourse and Sherwell is still the biggest 10th wicket partnership to win a test match.

Notes on the South African team:

Percy Sherwell: A wicket-keeper regarded as an expert at keeping to googly bowlers on matting. Played thirteen tests, all as captain. South Africa won five of them. The next Springbok captain to equal him was Jack Cheetham.

Gordon White: batsman and googly bowler. Played 17 tests with a highest score of 147. Plum Warner regarded him the best of the South African batsmen. Played soccer for South Africa. Killed in World War I.

Louis Tancred: opening batsman who played 14 tests with a highest score of 97, still the highest score by a South African in his test debut. Known for his ungainly crouch at the wicket. Regarded by some as South

Africa's best batsman. Good in England. Two brothers played cricket for South Africa.

Maitland Hathorn: stylish batsman in 12 tests with a highest score of 102, the second ever South African centurion. Good fielder. Played tennis for South Africa.

William Shalders: batsman in 12 tests with a highest score of 42. Useful bowler.

Jimmy Sinclair: still holds the record for the fastest test century by a South African – in 80 minutes vs the Australians at Newlands. He played 25 tests, scored over 1000 runs and took 63 wickets, a feat bettered only by Trevor Goddard and Aubrey Faulkner. Great fielder. Played rugby for South Africa and was a star soccer player. He died at the age of 37, a funeral attended by thousands

Aubrey Faulkner: the allrounder with the looks of a film star. The first South African to score a double century in a test. He played 25 tests, scored over 1700 runs and took 82 wickets with his googlies. In World War I he was awarded a DSO in Gallipoli. Settled in England where he died sadly.

Sibley Snooke: played 26 tests, scored over 1000 runs with a top score of 103 and took 35 wickets with 8/70 against Australia in Australia. Captain after Sherwell.

Ernie Vogler: took 64 wickets in 15 tests with his legspin and googlies. Top score 65. Good fielder. Played successfully for Kent for a season. Took 10 wickets in a Currie Cup innings, 36 wickets in a series and 12 wickets in a single test.

Reggie Schwartz: an Englishman who played 20 tests for South Africa, introduced the googly which South Africans used successfully,

Dave Nourse: took 55 wickets with a best of 6/47. Top test score 61 but scored a century at Lord's against a strong England XI. Played fly half for England before coming to South Africa. Killed in World War I. his names were really Arthur William. Played a record 45 tests in succession with a top score of 111. He scored over 2000 runs and took 41 wickets. Had enormous hands. Played his last test at 47. Came to South Africa from England as a soldier. Father of Dudley.

'GOD SAVE OIRELAND'

South Africa's first overseas rugby contact was with the British Isles and Ireland, the *fons et origo* of the game, and South Africans learnt reasonably quickly.

In 1891 the visitors swept through South Africa unbeaten, in 1896 they lost the last test, and in 1903 the South Africans won the series, as they did again in 1910.

When South Africans went abroad they headed for "Home". The start was quiet– defeat by Scotland, a draw with England, and victories over Ireland and Wales in 1906.

Two years before the First World War the Springboks toured Great Britain, Ireland and France. Their captain was Billy Millar, who nearly did not make it. He had played almost no rugby at SACS as a schoolboy and was crippled during the Anglo-Boer War when he joined up at the age of 17. It was believed that he would never have full use of his left arm and could in fact be an invalid for life. He became an exercise fanatic– boxing, tennis, golf, cricket, and competitive walking, and in 1903 he started playing rugby for Gardens.

In 1906 he played for Western Province and at the end of the year was in Paul Roos's team to tour the UK and Ireland, but only as a replacement for Bertie Mosenthal of Transvaal who withdrew before the tour got under way. He played 16 of the 29 matches on the tour, including one test– the one against England when he scored South Africa's try in a 3-all draw.

In 1910 he captained South Africa against Tommy Smyth's touring team, an interesting team which taught South Africa such functions as specialised half backs and loose forwards. CH "Cherry" Pilman became the first real loose forward to be seen in South Africa. He was only 20 at the time.

Billy Millar missed the first test on that tour because he could not get off from work. But it was not work or injuries that nearly kept him out of the team to Europe in 1912. The reason had no romance attached to it at all. Billy Millar was sent off the field playing for Gardens at Newlands. If things had gone any further, he would not have been able to play for Western Province – oh, for days of such virtue! – and would not have made the Springbok side. Apologies were made to the referee and the matter was dropped. Even so the selectors were not keen to have him but knew that he had the support of the SA Rugby Board who appointed the captain. The selectors, unlike the 1965 case when the Board vetoed the selectors' selection of Doug Hopwood, decided to do what they knew the Board wanted. Billy Millar went as captain, along with two other survivors of Paul Roos's side– Uncle Dobbin and Douggie Morkel.

This was the first of four successive Springbok teams to achieve a grand slam on a tour of the UK, compared with one All Black side and one Wallaby side. They struggled – just beating Llanelli and losing to Newport, to whom they gave a Springbok head, thus starting a tradition. The head is still in the cluhouse museum at Rodney Parade. London Counties (and that man Pillman) also beat them before they went north to Scotland.

The team, like other Springbok teams after it, had a strong sense of duty to its predecessors – to compensate for the errors of the past. Scotland had beaten the 1906 Springboks and Scotland must pay. Billy Millar's team won 16-0, a big score in those days. The next Sunday the Springboks met Ireland in Dublin and set a new world record.

Ireland were with England joint holders of the mythical Five Nations Championship that year. The match, played on 30th November, 1912, was due to be refereed by Frank Potter Irwin of England but he could not get across and was replaced by Mr J T Tulloch, a past president of the Scottish RU, who had refereed when the Springboks played Ireland and England in 1906. Johnny Tulloch broke down half way through the match and was replaced by Fred Gardener, the great Ulsterman who had played for Ireland at forward and – like Danie Craven and Gerrie Sonnekus – at half back and who had retired in 1909 with 21 caps.

The team which played for South Africa in all five Tests in 1905-6. back: B.de.R. Malraison (scorer), A.W. Nourse, S.J. Snooke, A.E.E. Vogler; middle: L.J. Tancred, J.H. Sinclair, R.O. Schwartz, P.W. Sherwell (captain), W.A. Shalders, C.M.H. Hathorn; front: G.A. Faulkner, G.C. White

South African K.K. McArthur does a victory lap after winning the Marathon at the 1912 Olympic Games in Stockholm

The South African team in the United Kingdom 1935. back: A.D. Nourse, E.L. Dalton, A.B.C. Langton, R.J. Crisp, D.S. Tomlinson, K.G. Viljoen, R.J. Williams; middle: A.J. Bell, C.L. Vincent, H.F. Wade (captain), S.J. Snooke (manager), H.B. Cameron, I.J. Siedle, B. Mitchell; front: X.C. Balaskas, E.A.B. Rowan

Above: The only conversion Gerry Brand was successful with in the deciding test of 1937 in New Zealand. But it did not matter as the Springboks won 17-6

Below: Dai Williams bursts across the line for the fourth try during the momentous third test at Eden Park in 1937

The man to tell the story of the match is Billy Millar:

In consequence of our thorough victory over Scotland, the newspaper critics, who previously had not been very generous in their opinions, came right over to our side. The *Morning Post* said that never since 1893 had the Scottish forwards been so roughly handled, and the *Sportsman* forecasted that if we kept up this form we would prove superior to every British fifteen brought against us – and the forecast happened to turn out correct.

Having got over the Scottish hurdle, our next important match was with Ireland, at Dublin, whom we licked by 38 points to nil. We played inspired football, and the Irishmen, who were weak in defence, were well-nigh annihilated by our fast, piercing forwards. The ground was bone dry, and one ran many risks of broken legs.

I shall never forget the reception we got from the Irish forwards. No sooner had the whistle sounded than they came down upon us. The forwards broke loose from their own 25, and fell upon us like a tornado. Fred Luyt tried to stem the tide, but he was brought down: MacHardy also tried, but he was sent sprawling lengthways.

However, Gerhard Morkel and Richard Luyt between them managed to repulse this violent forward drive. Right on top of this we had to face another onslaught, but this attack proved the undoing of the Irish. Fred Luyt whipped the ball from an Irish forward's foot, as he was driving through and sent it out to Dobbin. This movement started in our own "25," and away went our backs in full cry. Jack Morkel passed out to Dick Luyt, and the latter transferred to Stegmann.

The big wing, with 75 yards to cover before he reached his goal, dashed away in full flight, and beat his opposing three for speed. Dicky Lloyd tried to bar his path but failed, whilst the full-back who tried to get near the flying winger was completely "blotted out." It was a great try.

From this moment we took complete charge of the game, and within the next three or four minutes the referee whistled up three fine tries. As in the Scottish match, our forwards were playing the Irish at their own game; that is to say we met their wild tornado-like rushes in the loose with the same methods.

At the same time, however, we heeled from the scrums, and what with backs breaking away on daring raids, and our forwards, whenever necessary, rushing the Irishmen off their feet, we were well in the ascendancy.

Before half time, MacHardy scored three more tries. His first was the result of a 50 yards sprint, in which he upset the full-back who tried to stop him. We changed ends leading by 12 points to nil.

In the second half we were all over the Irishmen, and it is said we gave an exhibition of bewildering combination that has never been surpassed. Our backs were wonderful. True, they had every opportunity, seeing that we were masters in the front line. The Irishmen were absolutely bewildered by dazzling movements among our backs, the daring raids, and the unorthodoxy of it all. Fred Luyt's evolutions were well-nigh uncanny; he seemed to mesmerise his opponents.

I reckon this match would remain a nightmare for Irish Rugby men for many weeks, for every movement known to the game was daringly aggressive. Our backs, in fact, were on top of their form; they side-stepped wild attempts to tackle them and were as cool as the cucumber in evading those heavy rushes for which the Irish are famed. Then we forwards would have a turn in attack, and we handled almost as brilliantly as our backs. In fact, on this day's form it was a team of fifteen backs in action – some writer said the attacks were the most impudent ever seen.

The Irishmen were completely demoralised by the speed and accuracy of the attacks, and points were simply rushed up in the second half. Tedford, one of the greatest forwards Ireland has produced, said to me after the game: "This is a magnificent team of yours; why, your best 1906 side was not a patch on it, and what forwards!"

The Irish Press remarked that they never had any idea that a team could be made to operate in such a concerted manner. One paper commenting on the defeat, said, "The crowd came to see Ireland win; they saw Ireland win – the toss, and that was the only consolation from kick-off to "no side." Never has a good International side – not a weak one – been so utterly outclassed. What tremendous strides the game must have made in South Africa in those six years, when they can send out a team at length it can be written without exaggeration, "Here is a team superior in every way to the All Blacks of 1905.'"

There is no doubt about it that we surpassed ourselves this Saturday at Dublin. At the same time, in fairness to the defeated side, their task, trying to stave off attacks on a ground that was hard with frost, was not to be envied.

Chris Greyvenstein in *Springbok Saga* recalls another less orthodox Irish view of the match:

David McDonigal, a well known referee who settled in Cape Town in later years, saw the Lansdowne slaughter as a boy and he gave a most amusing if not always strictly correct, description of what it was like to be Irish that day.

"How optimistic we were!", he wrote. "Did we not remember that Paul Roos and his male beauty chorus had only just succeeded in beating us in 1906? And were we not given to understand that the 1906 Springboks were better than the 1912 variety? And had we not got the great Dickey Lloyd, the nippy Harry Read, the elusive Jeb Minch and the untiring Billy Burgess? What was there to be afraid of?

"Alas, what vain optimism. Ireland won the toss – it was the only thing we won that afternoon – and South

Africa kicked off. The ball was fumbled and went into touch near our "25". From the lineout there was a scrum. I distinctly saw the ball heeled cleanly into the hands of the waiting half, and the next thing I saw was a gentleman called Stegmann taking long strides up the touch-line and scoring behind the posts. He was a Springbok sprightly springing, or, as they say in Ireland, "Away he went, leppin' like a hare".

That was only the beginning and I think it best to draw a veil over the rest of that awful day. I well remember a remark passed by a friend of mine from far-away Kerry. The Springboks had rattled up some 20 points and Ireland were kicking off for the umpteenth time. During that moment of waiting, my friend exclaimed: "*Dearly beloved brethren, let us join in singing God Save Oireland, for it's destroyed we are, entoirely!*"

When we were walking away from the ground I happened to say "Well, anyhow, it was a glorious exhibition of rugby."

My friend replied: "*Bedad, me bhoy, that wasn't rugby at all. At laste, if it was, heaven alone knows what we've been playing these past years!*"

A cartoon published in a Dublin newspaper the day after the game showed Billy Millar eating 38 pieces of shamrock while Dickie Lloyd, drawn as a sad-looking Irish terrier, is sitting up, begging for a piece. The caption read: "And so the poor dog got none!"

Some of the records of that day in Dublin still stand. Ten remains the highest number of tries the Springboks have scored in a test, and it remains the only test in which two Springboks scored a hat-trick of tries, and they were the wings to boot. It was a good day to be a wing that day – a Springbok wing, that is.

The Springboks themselves broke the other record of the day – nearly 40 years later when they beat Scotland 44-0 at Murrayfield and raised the winning margin for a test match from 38 to 44. It still is the real world record, despite what statisticians, seemingly eager to get South Africa out of the record books, like to say about "funny" matches like Ireland versus Romania and New Zealand versus Italy, Fiji, and Japan.

Evelyn Edgar "Boot" McHardy of the Orange Free State was the first of the wings to score a hat-trick. He played in five tests and scored six tries. Jan Stegmann, whose brother Anton scored a try against Ireland in 1906, scored five tries in five tests. He hurdled for Scotland while studying dentistry at Edinburgh University.

The carnage of the First World War ended rugby internationals for some time. In that war several of the players who met on the tour of 1912-3 fought and some died, many died. Amongst them were Billy Burgess of Ireland and Jackie Morkel and the tough forward, Septimus Ledger of South Africa, who had played in the Dublin test.

There were only two tries scored when the Springboks played England at Tickenham, one by Jackie Morkel and the other, a brilliant effort in the first minute, by Ronnie Poulton (later known as Poulton Palmer), both of whom died on active service. (Poulton's try was the only one against the Springboks in the four tests that year).

Jackie King, who played for Somerset West for three years before returning to England, was also in the England side that day. He was killed in France. Morkel and Thompson played against Wales when Billy Geen marked Stegmann. Geen was killed in Belgium.

It was the Scottish match which took the heaviest toll. Three South Africans who played then were to be killed – Jackie Morkel, Ledger and Gerald Thompson. More than half the Scottish side beaten by the Springboks paid with their lives – Fred Turner, the captain, Walter Sutherland, Lewis Robertson, James Pearson, David Howie, Patrick Blair, David Bain, and Mike Dickson.

Amongst other rugby internationals with South African connections were the following: Reggie Schwartz (England), who played cricket for South Africa; Toby Moll of Transvaal who played for the Springboks in 1910; Basil Maclear who ran 75 yards to score a try for Ireland against the 1906 Springboks; Darkie Sivright who toured South Africa in

1903 and was in the Scottish team which beat the 1906 Springboks in Glasgow; John Williams (Wales) who played against Paul Roos's team and scored a splendid try for Cardiff against them; Charlie Pritchard and Dick Thomas who were in the Welsh pack in 1906; two members of the 1910 team to South Africa, Eric Milroy of Scotland and Philip Waller of Wales who later settled in Johannesburg; a group who fought in the Anglo-Boer War – David Gallagher who captained the first All Blacks, and the England players Billy Nanson, Charles Wilson, Ronnie Lagden and Alexander Todd who toured South Africa in 1896 with Johnny Hammond's team; some who played against the Springboks in the UK in 1912 such as Alfred Manyard (England) for Cambridge, Bob Pillman, Cherry's brother, who was in the London Counties pack which beat Millar's side, and Francis Oakley, the England scrum half, who played for Army and Navy. And then a quartet of internationals who went to school at Bishops in the Cape – Mike Dickson and "Beak" Steyn of Scotland who both played for Oxford against Millar's team, Reggie Hands (England), and Arthur Burdett who toured with Paul Roos's team.

Billy Millar did not come home unscathed from his second war either. He was severely wounded and returned virtually one-armed. But he managed to play golf and in 1924 he refereed the last two internationals when Cove-Smith's team toured.

He remembered the dead. "When one thinks of those splendid fellows, who played rugby, and who also played a great game in the same grand spirit when they paid the great price, one often ponders the reason of it all. Anyhow theirs was not to reason why. Playing for a bigger team in a greater game they gladly, and imbued with the real team spirit of Rugby in a national sense, gave their all. God rest their souls, gallant gentlemen all!"

I have strayed from that glorious test played at Lansdowne Road in Dublin before all the nastiness occurred. It was certainly one of the greatest achievements in the history of South African sport. It was good that Billy Millar made it after all.

STOCKHOLM 1912

The Olympic Games, founded with such purity of intention, have been bedevilled by controversy. This is true of South Africa's unique Olympic achievement, strangely at the first Olympics free of ontroversy – 1912 in Stockholm. There have not been many since then that have been wholly happy.

It's all sad because Baron de Coubertin had the best of motives, and yet it he had not been as determined a man as he was, the games would have been scuppered by pettiness and political wrangling long before we got to the harsh horror of political interference which started at Berlin and, after the brief interludes of the post-war recovery in London in 1948, the stability of Helsinki in 1952, and the really happy Olympics in Tokyo in 1964, there have been the fighting at Melbourne in 1956, the massacre in Mexico City just before the Olympics there with all the problems of thin air at high altitude, the Palestinian madness in Munich in 1972 and since then governmental use of the Olympic games for all sorts of political statements.

We must not think of the origins as innocent. There was opposition to Coubertin's idea, and the French did not relish competing with Germans and at one stage with the British as well. But the first modern Olympics in Athens was fairly enthusiastic for the 311 athletes (230 Greeks) who took part. Paris was a disappointment, St Louis in 1904 a farce, and in London (of all places) officials were accused of cheating in 1908.

Stockholm in 1912 as a delight. The city was beautiful with its waterfront, the sun shone, and the stadium with its cinder track was magnificent. Problems were minor.

The athletes got on well in a spirit which gave Coubertin pleasure. There was then no Olympic village, and part of the fun was visiting the American contingent who stayed on their transatlantic liner down in the harbour. There were 3889 athletes from 28 countries. Ten of them were South Africans who lived in a boarding house, hungry most of the time.

The marathon had not been an event at the ancient Greek Olympic Games though the run is Greek and famous. Pheidippides it was who brought the good news of victory over the Persians from Marathon to Athens and died doing so. It was only fitting that there be marathon in the modern Olympics, which started in Athens in 1896. To the delight of the Greeks a Greek, Spyros Louis won. King George I of Greece was so pleased that he allowed him to name his present. Spyros Louis chose a horse and cart. In that marathon only one non-Greek, Gyuala Kellner of Hungary finished. The marathon was an amateur affair, but it did capture popular imagination.

In Paris the marathon, run in great heat through the streets of the city, was won by a Frenchman – Michel Theato. And in St Louis the marathon was won by an American. The marathon typified the farce of the Olympics of that year when fewer than 100 non-Americans took part.

Fred Lord came in first and was acclaimed as the winner, presented to Alice Roosevelt, daughter of the president, and then disqualified for travelling part of the way on a truck. Instead Thomas Hicks of the USA was proclaimed the winner with the assistance of sulphate of strychnine and cognac in days when nobody worried about drugging athletes.

Running in that Olympic marathon were three South Africans: W B Harris and two Zulus whose names are recorded as Lenthauw and Yamasani, almost certainly not their real names. The Zulus were possibly part of a dancing troupe in St Louis at the time. Lentauw, after a detour when a dog chased him, came ninth, Yamasani was 124, and Harris failed to finish. This was South Africa's first entry into the Olympic marathon.

At the London Olympics, South Africa came close to a gold for the marathon run from Windsor Castle to the stadium in Shepherd's Bush and which fixed the distance at 26 miles 385 yards (42,195m), Pheidippides's run. The marathon was run on the final day, the hottest of the British summer, and ended before 90 000 people in the stadium. Second to John Hayes of the USA, the first non-native to win the marathon, was Charles Hefferson of South Africa. In Stockholm the South Africans were to improve on that achievement and their feat has not been equalled since.

There were 68 entries for the marathon in Stockholm, from 20 countries, including four South African's – Chris Gitsham, KK McArthur, Leonard Richardson, who did not actually run, and ACC St Norman who did not finish. Originally only McArthur was chosen for the marathon but Gitsham had done well in coming second in the Polytechnic Harriers Marathon in London when the team were staying there preparing for the Olympics.

The manager of the South African team was H B Keartland, for many years sports editor of *The Star,* a man with an eye for a promising sportsman. He got a shock on the Saturday night before the marathon when one of the team told him that Chris Gitsham had gone off to run the marathon course! Bert Keartland got a taxi and caught up with Gitsham after he had done some 18km of the course. Gitsham was whisked off the road into the taxi and back to the boarding house. His explanation? He was out to see if he could run the course. He could, no doubt about that!

The Swedes had had problems finding a suitable course. They eventually decided to start in the stadium, run to Sollentuna, turn and come back to finish in the stadium, just under 2km short of what is now the standard distance.

It was a hot Sunday in Stockholm, 14th July, 1912, and they started the race in the worst of the heat at twelve minutes to two. The road was dusty though big stones had been removed to make it easier. Traffic was forbidden during the race and a hundred policemen and three hundred soldiers were there to see that the athletes were in no way hampered by unwarranted intrusion.

There were control points with medical help and race advice, and there was a radio connection with the stadium so that the crowd there could be told of the progress of the race. Ther runners were allowed no seconds, and Bert Keartland and the rest of the South African contingent could but sit with the rest of the big crowd in the stadium and watch the information posted from time to time.

Leading at the start were the Swede, Ahlgren and the Finn Tatu Kolehmainen, brother of Hannes who was the star of the 1912 Olympics and who would win the marathon in 1920.

After 5km they reached the first control point at Stocksund with Kolehmainen in the lead from Ahlgren and the Italian Carlo Speroni. The first 5km had taken 29 minutes. Gitsham and McArthur were close behind the leaders at this stage.

There were 10km to the next control point at Tureberg. Kohlehmainen was first there at eighteen minutes to three with the two South Africans in myrtle green 13 seconds behind him. The first 15km had taken 54 mins. Fred Lord of Britain was fourth with Ahlgren and Sigge Jacobsson of Sweden following and Speroni of Italy further back.

Kolehmainen was determined to "kill" the rest of the field but little Chris Gitsham, who had warmed up well the night before, was not to be shaken off and he stayed at Finn's shoulder for some 7km before he went ahead at the turning point which Githam reached at 3.00.40, 25m ahead of Kolehmainen. Ken McArthur was in third place just under a minute behind, followed by Lord, Speroni, Ahlgren, Jacobsson, and Jim Corkery of Canada who was one of the pre-race favourites. The two leaders did not stop for refreshment in the heat but those following did.

Back the runners came, the first three in the same order but with Ahlgren dropping back and Speroni and Jacobsson passing Lord. And an American Indian, Lewis Tewanima, was coming through the field.

At Tureberg there was less than a second between Gitsham, Kolehmainen, and McArthur. But the South Africans were better used to the heat and before Stocksund, Kolehmainen pulled to the side of the road and dropped out of the race.

The two men in green were now out on their own, more than a minute ahead of the field. And is is at this stage that the first steps were taken which would lead to controversy.

Ken McArthur, the older and the heavier of the two men, was struggling while Gitsham was running freely. Gitsham, in the comradely spirit which was more likely to be prevalent then than now, stayed with his team-mate, encouraging him, running him through the pain. For 4km they ran together, stride for stride.

Back they came to Stocksund, the last control point before the stadium. Gitsham and McArthur got there just after 4. But the rest changed remarkably. In third place, was Gaston Strobino of the USA, who was moving up the field. Then came Jacobsson, James Duffy of Canada, Speroni, and a clutch of other Americans. Lord had dropped back. Gitsham and McArthur would have been told the race situation. 5km to go.

In the stadium expectancy grew in the crowd, especially amongst the South Africans and other contingents from the Commonwealth. Then cheering grew and came closer.

Down the hilly country road lying to the north of the stadium came a man in green, an Irishman running for South Africa, Ken McArthur from Potchefstroom, and he was running alone, tired, glancing over his shoulder in anxiety which calmed when he was told that Chris Gitsham, his team-mate who had run him through much of his pain, was some five minutes behind. Gitsham had stopped to drink at a roadside fountain, and McArthur had stopped with him. Suddenly cramp had struck Gitsham's legs, and McArthur had run on.

Into the stadium, at an easy pace, came McArthur and the crowd roared. Bert Keartland up in the stand was so choked that he could not tell the pressmen which one of his team it was that was leading, lapping around the stadium with nobody else in sight.

An official ran out onto the track with a laurel wreath, bumped McArthur in trying to put it on, and the runner staggered. Bert Keartland leapt off the stand, brushed aside two soldiers who tried to stop him, and dashed onto the track to knock the official out of the way.

In the London marathon in 1908 the first man home was an Italian Dorando Pietri who had been disqualified after coming in first because an official had helped him when he arrived in agony at the stadium.

Garlanded McArthur turned the last bend, enjoying the adulation of the crowd. As he did so, Chris Gitsham entered the stadium, mush fresher looking than McArthur.

McArthur in triumph breasted the tape and dropped to the ground to be attended by doctors. 58 seconds later Gitsham finished in second place. And he was angry. He went straight up to the winner and said, "You dirty dog." Bert Keartland grabbed him and wrapped his hand around his mouth to prevent a scene. Gitsham felt that McArthur had abondoned him after he had stuck by McArthur at McArthur's request. The crowd continued to applaud the two South Africans, a policeman from Potchefstroom and a miner from Germiston, the only two men from one country to have come first and second in the Olympic marathon.

It was the end of McArthur's career, but Gitsham was to race at the next Olympics – in Antwerp in 1920 when Hannes Kolehmainen won. Gitsham was unplaced.

Half of the Stockholm field did not finish, and one, Francisco Lazaro of Portugal, collapsed near the finish and was taken to the Seraphim Hospital where he died early on the Monday morning.

The Greek, Spyros Louis, who won the first marathon, was given a horse and cart; Kenneth Kane McArthur was given a plot of land in Kock Street, Potchefstroom where he built a house for himself and his wife, Joe – Johanna Jacoba Christina Brand of Barbeton who used to ride her bicycle next to him as he trained.

Ken McArthur came to South Africa from Northern Ireland to join Baden Powell's South African Constabulary at the end of the Anglo-Boer War. He was stationed in Potchefstroom where he met his wife-to-be, who first thought of him as a Horse-face!

McArthur's athletics career began in South Africa where rugby, tennis, and soccer also claimed his time. He was 1,88 m tall and weighed 77 kg – a big man for a marathon athlete.

The people of Potchefstroom were proud of him. They named an athletics stadium after him and kept his trophies and medals in their museum. Also there is his Stockholm number, 613. His career effectively lasted from 1906 to 1912. He was just over thirty at the time of the marathon in Stockholm.

Constable "Marathon Mac" MacArthur was on his bicycle patrol when Colonel Izak Meyer of Potchefstroom drove up in his horse-drawn cart and suggested that McArthur attach himself on the cart to make things easier. The bicycle's wheel hit a rock, and McArthur was thrown. He injured his foot and ended his athletics career which was problably at an end anyway.

After leaving the SAP, McArthur was head of the mine police at Crown Mines. On 13th June, 1960 at the age of 78 he died in Potchefstroom where he is buried.

The result of the 1912 Marathon run in Stockholm, Sweden:

1. KK McArthur (South Africa)   2hr 36:54,8
2. CW Gitsham (South Africa)   2hr 37:52,0
3. G Strobino (USA)   2hr 38:42,4
4. A Sockalexis (USA)   2hr 42:07,9
5. James Duffy (Canada)   2hr 42:18,8
6. Sigge Jacobsson (Sweden)   2hr 43:24,9
7. J J Gallagher (USA)   2hr 44:19,4
8. Joseph Erxloben (USA)   2hr 45:17,2
9. Richard Piggott (USA)   2hr 46:40,7
10. Joseph Forshaw (USA)   2hr 49:49,4
11. E Fabre (Canada)   2hr 50:36,2
12. C H de Mar (USA)   2hr 52:11,4
13. Bossiere (France)   2hr 51:06,6
14. H Green (Great Britain)   2hr 52:11,4
15. W C Forsyth (Canada)   2hr 52:23,0
16. L Tewanima (USA)   2hr 52:41,4
17. H Smith (USA)   2hr 52:53,8
18. T H Lilley (USA)   2hr 59:35,4
19. A Townsend (Great Britain)   3hr 00:00,5
20. F Kwieton (Austria)   3hr 01:48,0
21. F Lord (Great Britain)   3hr 01:39,2
22. J Westberg (Sweden)   3hr 02:05,2
23. A G Simonsen (Norway)   3hr 04:59,4

24. C Anderson (Sweden)   3hr 06:13,0
25. E W Lloyd (Great Britain)   3hr 09:25,0
26. H P Sakelloropoulos (Greece)   3hr 11:37,0
27. H Dahlberg (Sweden)   3hr 13:32,2
28. I Lundberg (Sweden)   3hr 16:35,2
29. J Christensen (Denmark)   3hr 21:57,4
30. O Laodal (Denmark)   3hr 21:57,6
31. O Karpati (Hungary)   3hr 25:31,6
32. C Nilsson (Sweden)   3hr 26:56,4
33. E Rath (Austria)   3hr 27:03,8
34. O Osen (Norway)   3hr 36:35,6

Amongst those who did not finish were runners from Australia, Bohemia, Chile, Italy, Japan, Russia, and Servia. Finland was then a part of Csarist Russia and not allowed to have its own flag. When Hannes Kolehmanien won one of his three gold medals and the Russian flag was hoisted he said, "I would almost not have won than see that flag up there."

A RUBBER IS WON

South African cricketers first toured England in 1894. The last tour was in 1965. In that time 13 Springbok teams went to England. Only two won the series, and they were thirty years apart.

In the Thirties there was a world depression. In South Africa there was a depression, but the cricketers started quite well. There was the beginning of a transition from matting to turf and, despite all sorts of squabbles about captaincy, the Springboks won the five-test series 1-0. But then depression set in, when they set off for a 5-0 defeat in the series in Australia at a time when the Aussies had players called Don Bradman, who scored four consecutive test centuries against the Springboks, Woodfull, Ponsford, Clarrie Grimmett and Bill O'Reilly, Stan McCabe, and Bert Ironmonger. It was not a contest, which must have made the return trips in 1952 and 1963 all the sweeter for Ken Viljoen.

In 1935 Herbie Wade captained a Springbok team on a 40-match tour of the UK. There were a lot of young players in the team – Dudley Nourse and Eric Rowan amongst them. They did well, losing only twice. At Trent Bridge, the Springboks followed on and were saved by the rain. But then they thumped Yorkshire when Jock Cameron got a century, including 30 off an over from Verity, and Xenephon Balaskas took wickets with his leg spin. And so to Lords for the second test.

England, captained by Bob Wyatt, had names such as Hammond, Sutcliffe, Leyland, Ames, and Verity to suggest that they were no mean side.

Funny things happen to cricket wickets. They wear, they crack, they get wet, they crumble and, if you are in Durban, they get affected by the tide. Lords for that test had been infested with "leather jackets", crane fly larva. The leather jackets chewed away patches of grass, and it was a good toss to win.

South Africa left out Cyril Vincent, their most experienced spinner, but Herby Wade won the toss and batted.

Louis Duffus, doyen of South African cricket writers, was there and recalls:

> On the Saturday afternoon of June 29, 1935 the applause of 35 000 spectators echoed over Lord's as Eric Rowan was caught at the wicket off Hedley Verity. The scoreboard showed that at the first day of their second test match in England South Africa were 98 for 4.
>
> In those days the two of us who represented the South African Press were welcome to spend any time we liked in the dressingroom. Before the sound of distant clapping had died down we saw Jock Cameron stand up in his pads and hold out his bat.
>
> He caressed it playfully and murmured with soft appeal, "Are you going to be a good pal today?"
>
> With that he jerked on his cap, opened the door, passed down the stairs into the Long Room and out into the sunlit area of the sacred ground. We little knew what a profound part in the history of South African cricket destiny held in store for him, and the team.
>
> He was of medium height, strongly built – everything about him, legs, shoulders and forearms portrayed solidity and strength. His natural mien was a little grim. Even when about to perpetrate some outrageous piece of horse-play he wore a serious expression, like a mask.
>
> I wonder what passed through his mind as he faced up to Verity? Only a week before he had plastered him in one of the memorable big-hitting feats of cricket. Perhaps Verity was still shaking from the indignity of that ordeal for when Cameron had scored only 11 the lefthander lost his usual immaculate length and bowled a full-toss. Cameron pulled it over the boundary for six.
>
> He was the most scientific and calculating of the South African big hitters I have known. He would tap the good length deliveries with the gentleness of a girl,

but when he had decided upon the ball to be hit he punched it with fury, and a superb sense of balance. A command of fine judgment, and patience, were the essence of his techinque. Those who knew his style watched and waited in eager suspense for the precious moments of onslaught. Something of the same restraint and exact timing are to be seen in the present-day batting of Mike Procter.

Quick to assess an over-pitched ball from Langridge he lifted it high into the crowd sitting in the stand below the effigy of Father Time. With successive strokes he hit the legspin bowler Tom Mitchell for 6 and 4 and once he moved well to the off-side of the stumps to swing him magnificently to the midfield rails.

His innings was interrupted, as the players paused for drinks, by the arrival of King George V and the presentation of the teams and it was broken again by the tea interval. He lost two partners in Herby Wade and Eric Dalton but nothing disturbed the rhythm of his exhilarating display. At one stage he scored 58 out of 60 in half an hour.

I felt the thrill of his innings perhaps more than most onlookers, for during its course I had to telephone to Johannesburg to give Saturday night readers of the Argus Company's Sporting Editions the latest news of the match. It was the first time the trans-Atlantic long distance telephone had been used in the history of reporting in South Africa.

At the rate of £1 a minute I was able to dictate comment from each of the captains, Wade and Bob Wyatt, and to add: "There is no need for alarm at South Africa's poor score although some of the batsmen were disappointing. The wicket is bad. England will have to fight for runs. Cameron is playing the innings of his life . . ."

He had reached the stage when he seemed certain to record his first test century when the fast bowler Nichols with the new ball, beat him fairly with a delivery that whipped in off the pitch and crashed into the stumps.

Having scored a glorious 90 out of 126 in 105 minutes with three sixes and six fours, he walked back to the pavilion to an onforgettable ovation. It would have been typical of his character if he had patted his bat as he reached the dressingroom and murmured, "thank you pal".

The last four batsmen scored only 12 runs between them and South Africa were all out for 228.

South Africa's score was not really much, so it seemed, to cause the grand men of English cricket any sleeplessness on the free Sunday which followed. That Sunday – bless those innocent days – the Springboks took tea with the King and Queen at Buckingham Palace.

On Monday the wicket helped the spinners and Balaskas took 5/49, and England were all out for 198.

Often South African cricket has done well when it has batsmen willing to go for the runs. Bruce Mitchell was not that kind of batsman but his innings was without doubt a match-winner. He went in first and was still there when Herby Wade declared at 278/7. Eric Rowan helped with 44 but the biggest partnership was that between Mitchell and Chud Langton. They put on 101 for the seventh wicket, a record broken in the fifth test of the same series when Langton and Eric Dalton put on 137 and made the series safe for South Africa.

Mitchell's score was then the highest by a South African in a test in England and he managed it despite a sore eye. E.W. Swanton has this to say of the innings: "Bruce Mitchell truly came into his own when South Africa batted again, batting five and a half hours for 164, an innings marked by un-wearying patience and a quietly efficient technique. Mitchell stands up to the acid test of class – he can be extremely slow without being boring. He gave no catch in his innings and however sharply the ball turned, or however little it rose, he rarely failed to meet it with a smooth, unhurried stroke. The bad ones he hit with safety and profit."

England were left $4\frac{3}{4}$ hours to score 309 runs, and they batted down to Verity at number 10.

This time Chud Langton was the chief destroyer. He got Sutcliffe, Hammond, Ames, and Holmes, the pride of England's batting for 31 runs. Bob Crisp got two and Balaskas four to end with match figures of 9/103. England were all out by tea for 151, and South Africa had won her first test in England.

There were still three tests to play, but in that summer of three-day tests and funny weather the three ended in draws, though not without some resolute batting by the Springboks, especially Wade, Dalton, Mitchell, Nourse, Viljoen, Cameron, and Rowan.

If the tour was happy and successful, the return was marred by great sorrow. On the voyage home, Jock Cameron, the team's vice-captain and a most popular and respected cricketer, contracted enteric fever. He died in Johannesburg on 2nd November, 1935 at the age of 30.

Scorecard:
England vs South Africa at Lord's on 29th June, 1st & 2nd July, 1935.

South Africa   1st Innings
B Mitchell lbw b Nichols	30
IJ Siedle b Mitchell	6
EAB Rowan c Farrimond b Verity	40
AD Nourse b Verity	3
HF Wade c Hammond b Langridge	23
HB Cameron b Nichols	90
EL Dalton c & b Langridge	19
X Balaskas b Verity	4
ABC Langton c Holmes b Hammond	4
RJ Crisp n.o.	4
AJ Bell b Hammond	0
Extras	5
Total	278

Bowling:	O	M	R	W
Nichols	21	5	47	2
Wyatt	4	2	9	0
Hammond	5.3	3	8	2

Mitchell	20	3	71	1
Verity	28	10	61	3
Langridge	13	3	27	2

England 1st Innings

RES Wyatt c Nourse b Dalton	53
Sutcliffe lbw b Bell	3
Leyland b Balaskas	18
Hammond b Dalton	27
Ames b Balaskas	5
ERT Holmes c Bell b Balaskas	10
Langridge, James c Mitchell b Balaskas	27
Farrimond b Balaskas	13
Nichols c Cameron b Langton	10
Verity lbw b Langton	17
Mitchell n.o.	5
Extras	10
Total	193

Bowling:	O	M	R	W
Crisp	8	1	32	0
Bell	6	0	16	1
Langton	21.3	3	58	2
Balaskas	32	8	49	5
Dalton	13	1	33	2

South Africa 2nd Innings

B Mitchell n.o.	164
IJ Siedle c Farrimond b Mitchell	13
EAB Rowan lbw b Nichols	44
AD Nourse b Verity	2
HF Wade b Verity	0
HB Cameron c Ames b Mitchell	3
EL Dalton c Wyatt b Verity	0
ABC Langton c & b Hammond	44
Extras	8
Total	278 for 7 wickets (declared)

44

Bowling:	O	M	R	W
Nichols	18	4	64	1
Wyatt	4	2	2	0
Hammond	14.4	4	26	1
Mitchell	33	5	93	2
Verity	38	16	56	3
Langridge	10	4	19	0
Holmes	4	2	10	0

England 2nd Innings

RES Wyatt B Balaskas	16
Sutcliffe lbw b Langton	38
Leyland b Crisp	4
Hammond c Cameron b Langton	27
Ames lbw b Langton	8
ERT Holmes b Langton	8
Langridge, James lbw b Balaskas	17
Farrimond b Crisp	13
Nichols n.o.	7
Verity c Langton b Balaskas	8
Mitchell st Cameron b Balaskas	1
Extras	4
Total	151

Bowling:	O	M	R	W
Crisp	15	4	30	2
Bell	12	3	21	0
Langton	11	3	31	4
Balaskas	27	3	54	4
Mitchell	2	0	11	0

Result: South Africa won by 157 runs. The English players who have initials are amateurs.

45

FIVE TRIES TO NIL

"When South Africa plays New Zealand, consider your country at war." Those are the words of Boy Louw, who had spent his war as a bombardier in the Western Desert, in the Springbok dressingroom prior to the first test in 1949. There is no doubt that tests between Springboks and All Blacks are special. They rise above all others in intensity and skill. They are in fact the real test of rugby ability. All others are second rate.

It was evident in the early part of this century and certainly by the outbreak of World War I that there were two powers in world rugby which stood head and shoulders above the others and that there was little to choose between them – New Zealand and South Africa. Only matches between them, inconveniently situated in those days before air travel, would decide who could best lay claim to being, at that particular time, the top of the rugby world. The Lions have roared briefly and the Wallabies have hopped occasionally but it is true still today that the real test of rugby strength lies in matches between South Africa and New Zealand.

Immediately after the 1st World War the New Zealand Armed Forces toured South Africa. They did not play tests but they won 11 of their fifteen matches with victories over Transvaal, Western Province, Natal, Eastern Province and Orange Free State amongst them. They served notice that New Zealand rugby was strong.

The Springboks went to Australia (no tests) and New Zealand in 1921. Theo Pienaar's team, on a tour of 24 matches in more than four months with many injuries, shared three-match series 1-1 when the last test, with the rain bucketing down, ended scoreless. In all they lost twice – to the All Blacks and to Canterbury.

"Drawing," said that famous New Zealander, Tom Pearce, "is like kissing your sister."

The first series ended in a draw and after it the toast was "Till we meet again." Quietly confident men on both sides raised their glasses.

The next meeting was in 1928 in South Africa, this time for four tests, and this time South Africa had Bennie Osler, the first of South Africa's match-winning fly halves.

The All Blacks had a rough ride, losing six and drawing one of their 23 matches. And when the Springboks thrashed them 17-0, still the biggest hiding the Springboks have given the All Blacks, at Kingsmead in Durban, it looked as if the series was won. After all, who would beat Bennie who scored 14 points that day?

Bennie Osler was not that dominant in the rest of the series, and there followed victory for the All Blacks by a point at Ellis Park, defeat by five points in Port Elizabeth and with South Africa poised for victory they brought Mark Nicholls in to fly half, and in the rain and mud of Newlands he outplayed Bennie Osler on his home turf, and the series was indeed drawn.

Again they smiled and raised their glasses. "Till we meet again."

Again would be in New Zealand in 1937 at a time when South African rugby was riding the crest of the wave, but at the end of the Bennie Osler era. There had been great forwards in those days – Phil Mostert, Boy en Fanie Louw, Philip Nel, Bert Kipling, Ferdie Bergh, George Daneel, Lucas Strachan, André McDonald, and Manie Geere. But it was four years since they had played.

There was a North vs South match in Ellis Park, meant to serve as a trial. The selectors picked the teams, and the North won 25-16. The selectors were dissatisfied and called for a series of trials in Cape Town that April to which they invited 56 players plus a lot of local men to fill in. At the behest of Oubaas Markotter they did funny things like play John Apsey, the Springbok forward, at fly half and Howard Watt, another forward, at fullback while Fonnie van der Vyver played number eight. Tony Harris and Flappie Lochner played in the "fish-and-chips" trial on the first day, and worst of all, there was nobody who looked remotely like a Bennie Osler.

After the final trials, the selectors, led by Bill Schreiner who was a selector for forty years, went off to the Civil Service Club while the players went off to the Metropole Hotel to await their fate.

To the players waiting patiently at the hotel, the ordeal proved a nerve wracking one, as they sat in corners trimming their finger-nails with their teeth, gulping down stimulants to help to forget their anxiety, or strewing the carpets with cigarette ends as plentifully as autumn leaves.

There had been an official dinner at the hotel, and Mr. Twentyman Jones, who presided, tried to do something to drag out the proceedings and keep the minds of the men occupied, by calling upon those who thought they had been chosen to say why they would be chosen; and those, who considered themselves "out of it," to explain why they should be omitted.

It was well past 11 o'clock before Mr. Schreiner made his long awaited appearance. By that time the street outside the Hotel Metropole was choked up by enthusiasts who had been waiting for hours. Mr. Schreiner had to go to the first floor balcony facing the street so that the public as well as the players could hear the names as he announced them. Cheers punctuated the mention of every player, despite the fact that many of the loudest and most sincere in their applause, must have been disappointed players themselves.

The general feeling at the time was that the "if" factors in the side were the half-backs and the centre three-quarters, though it was appreciated that in favourable circumstances there was room for a lot of improvement among these paticular backs.

Philip Nel the Captain declared: "I think these players will mould into the greatest side I have ever known. The experience of the forwards is a splendid asset and should be a tremendous advantage in New Zealand. In spite of being a very heavy lot, they are remarkably fast. We shall be able to field a particularly mobile pack in every game. Many of the forwards can be played in alternate positions and that should prove a considerable factor during the had tour ahead of us."

"Apart from Brand, there are no backs with tremendous

48

reputations as outstanding stars. But they are men who, I am sure, will make reputations for themselves. They have every potentiality for developing into some of the greatest players we have ever seen. This should be a far greater team, as a team, than the 1931-2 side in Britain. I have every hope that they will develop into a remarkably efficient and smooth working machine."

The team chosen was: Gerry Brand, Freddie Turner, D O Williams, Pat Lyster, Jan Broodryk, Dendy Lawton, Louis Babrow, Johnny Bester Koffie Hofmeyr, Jimmy White, Flappie Lochner, Fonny van der Vyver, Tony Harris, Danie Craven, Pierre de Villiers, Ebbo Bastard, Ferdie Bergh, Ben du Toit, C B Jennings, Jan Lotz, Boy Louw, Harry Martin, Philip Nel, Roy Sherriff, Lucas Strachan, Mauritz van den Bergh, George van Reenen, and Howard Watt. The manager was Percy Day, his assistant (not, in those days, the coach) Alec de Villiers.

The captain was the 35-year-old Greytown farmer, Phillip Nel, his vice-captain Danie Craven, who many would have thought would have captained the side.

On the tour the manager and his assistant had virtually no say in the playing of the games. They did not even have a vote on the selection committee which consisted of Nel, Craven, Boy Louw, Gerry Brand and Lucas Strachan.

The team left for Australia on the "Ulysses". There to see them off was Paul Roos who had travelled up from Cape Town to Durban and who addressed the men with stirring words. "Let the spirit be the spirit of the Charge of the Light Brigade. "Theirs was not to reason why theirs was but to do or die." "And my final words to you are that you keep yourselves throughout the tour in the pink of condition, because you have a duty to perform first to your hosts who have invited you there, and secondly to your own country, which is sending you overseas. The message I bring to you from the South African Board is that you should go forth , my boys, and win your spurs."

Such stirring stuff suited the voyage on the "Ulysses", their Oddyssey to fame from which they would return heroes.

It wasn't easy to keep fit on board, and games were limited, especially as the only cricket ball plopped into the Indian to be followed by the only rugby ball. Most of the team took a turn at shovelling and stoking coal, though after the coal dust had been washed off and the novelty worn off, this became neither a popular nor anything like a regular game!

They roamed Australia, losing to New South Wales, but winning both tests, the second a dirty match. Australia had in their ranks men like Wild Bill Cerutti and Awesome Aub Hodgson. Not gentle men!

Then it was on to New Zealand and a triumphant progress up to the first test at Athletic Park in Wellington. The team's selectors, rather rudderless without an independent chairman, made mistakes. Danie Craven, through no engineering of his own, went to fly half. Philip Nel was left out and Boy Louw had a damaged chest. Only D O Williams emerged with credit as the New Zealanders surprised everybody in New Zealand by winning 13-7, a try apiece.

Stung by defeat the Springboks scored 131 points in the four matches before the second test, and this time there were wiser selections. Nel came back and Craven went to scrum half with Tony Harris at fly half. And Boy Louw was there. But Boy, that most loyal and serious of rugby men, was concussed during the game at a time when there were no subsitutes and stayed on to roam the field giggling. But the Springboks won to square the series. There were early shocks when Jack Sullivan scored two tries, one from an intercept to put the All Blacks up 6-0.

That brought them, via four more big wins, to the final test at Eden Park in Auckland. One to play, and everything to win.

Rugby ruled in Auckland that week, as the teams prepared for the decisive encounter which could at last break the empasse between the two teams.

The Springboks made one change – Flappie Lochner for the injured Jimmy White in the centre while the All Blacks changed four. One of the Springboks nearly did not play. For Louis Babrow the 25th September that year would be Yom Kippur. But the team were desperate. There was no replacement for Babrow. Babrow agonised and eventually came up with a bright solution.

"I'm a South African Jew, aren't I?" he asked his team mates. They agreed, unenthusiastically. "And South Africa is ten hours behind New Zealand isn't it?" Again they agreed. Then came the solution. "Well, that means the game will be over before it's Yom Kippur in South Africa. I play."

Two things, in pre-match planning, worked to South Africa's advantage. First of all the laws of the day allowed a team to opt for a scrum instead of a line-out, and South Africa had the stronger forwards and the All Blacks compounded their problems by ignoring scrumming in favour of a 2-3-2 formation with one forward acting as a "rover". They just weren't used to scrumming.

The other was mystique surrounding Craven's dive pass. People were in awe of its length.

Paul Roos sent the Springboks a cablegram with three words on it: "Skrum, skrum, skrum". He knew the tactics which could win.

They shoehorned 58 000 people into Auckland Park that day, a record until 61 000 got in to watch the 1956 Springboks. Since then they have altered the ground and its capacity is now 57 000. 58 000 was roughly a third of the whole population of Auckland, man, woman, and child.

In an Auckland street, a farmer stopped a Springbok half-back. He offered to wager his farm against a South African victory. Amongst the crowd were Maoris by the trainload from Rotorua. In the sulphur-heavy atmosphere of the geysers and the hot springs the Springboks had made many friends, as their successors of 1956 were to do some 19 years later. "We'll be at Eden Park to cheer for you," they declared, and at Eden Park they were. A Maori family named their newly born baby Gerry Brand.

The players were tight with nerves. Philip Nel, the Springbok captain, doubted whether test match rugby was any longer worth the while. It had become overbearingly serious, overpoweringly enmeshed in national pretige. And, in secret, the players practised a move based on Craven's dive-pass.

51

In the throng, as the players reached the ground, Danie
Craven espied a little old lady and made his way across to
her. "Would you like to see the Springboks play?" he asked.

"How can I?"

Craven pressed a player's complimentary ticket into her
hand, then moved away as tears welled in her eyes.

Mr J S King, of Wellington, had handled the second test
and was again the Springbok's choice for this one.

Reg Sweet describes the match:

> Nel had not long to wait to play his first card. New
> Zealand put the ball into touch, and he trotted up
> We'll scrum, New Zealand!" It was a voice of authority
> of a man who had forged a weapon which he knew was
> good and was about to put it to the test.
>
> South Africa won four scrums in a row. It was the
> shape of things to come. And from the fourth of these
> as Craven served Harris and Harris prepared to hand
> on to Lochner, Sullivan dashed forward as he had at
> Christchurch. Harris was alert, for the lesson of the
> second test, with Sullivan's intercept try, remained a
> bitter one.
>
> Fractionally, Harris withheld his pass and the fleeting
> chance of an intercept was gone – and Lochner, taking
> a high ball, steadied it on his shoulder without as much
> as stammering in his stride and plunged, like a falcon
> on its prey, through the breach the defence had left. On
> he raced and on . . . up to Taylor, waiting for his man,
> out to Babrow. And when Babrow dived across the All
> Blacks line the game was three minutes old precisely.
>
> What a start! What a crushing moral blow. What a
> chance, now, to exploit the advantage and to don the
> Rugby Crown. Brand missed the kick, but it hardly
> seemed to matter.
>
> Brand was off the line with a brace of penalties, then
> Trevathan, the All Black fly-half failed with one and
> later with another. Nel's eight shoved with a co-ordina-
> tion that could not be bettered. Lotz heeled with the
> sure touch of a man who knew his business in the

middle of the front, and he moved a former All Black to the observation that here was a player to whom South Africa should erect a monument. The ball came, and Craven and Harris went – in almost perfect harmony, safe in the assurance that outside of them were three-quarters who had already shown their mettle and who were poised to strike again.

Harris probed for an opening, then Lochner, and Craven worked the blind side. Mitchell strove for a breakthrough, but Lochner pulled him down. Sullivan it was whom the All Blacks missed now in the centre, and Sullivan was languishing on the wing. Williams slipped through, and Babrow followed suit. Here was a back division to put to the proof the finest defence in the world, and on this day New Zealand's fell somewhat below that order.

Now it was Babrow again, jinking through, then cracking on the pace as he worked out toward the right. Challenged, he kicked across and in perfect formation his forwards streamed downfield, positioned to a pinpoint for this very move: Bergh and "Boy" and Fanie Louw, Nel, Bastard and Van den Berg. It was more than human flesh could hold at bay. And Bergh, jubilantly clutching the ball to him as it dropped, was up to the line and over and the points were six, even as Babrow danced a jig of sheer delight and others followed suit. Brand converted, and then there were eight.

Not in their highest flights of fancy had the Springboks hoped for this. They were on top, they were going like clockwork. And now there were backs who urged Craven to employ the "secret" move as well. Might as well make a meal of it. But Craven stayed them. He felt the moment should be delayed; and in the first half, the chance did not recur.

New Zealand, picking up the pattern piecemeal, was putting on a better face. There was not a great deal to be done in the matter of Mitchell and Caughey, the two on whom such ambitious hopes were pinned. From the start they had been tackled into impotence. Mitchell

hurt a finger and was transferred to the wing, and fo
the present, at least, Caughey in the centre met with
little better fortune.

The scrums were still South Africa's in the proportion
of two to one, and on this basis it was the Springbok
who could call the tune. When Lambourn heeled fo
New Zealand, Hooper stab-punted and looked
dangerous, but there again was this fearsome pack and
Bergh, Bastard and Strachan drove New Zealand back
King whipped up his forwards and tried again. Turner
plunged into their midst and put the brake on.

Trevathan had his fourth kick for the posts – a
penalty, the better part of 50 yards and his hardest yet
This one flew straight and true, and its range was right
South Africa 8, New Zealand 3, and the All Blacks
flung themselves back in the fight with hope re-kindled.
Trevathan, Hooper and Caughey all tried as the ball
came back to them, the forwards showing a fire they
had lacked in the earlier stages. But the defence stood
its ground and 8-3 it remained at half-time, with the
finger of probability pointing clearly at South Africa.

Forty minutes left, 40 of the most vital minutes in the
story of test match Rugby; certainly the most significant
in all the 16 years of striving between All Blacks and
Springboks. Now it is the first minute of the second
half. Taylor has returned a fairly deep kick-off to near
half-way, on his right-hand touchline. Craven makes
his decision on the spur of the fleeting moment . . .the
move! What better instant than this one? If it works, he
reasons, the psychological advantage will be all South
Africa's.

Harris is aghast. The forwards pack down, and
Craven motions him to stand off farther. Harris is
worried, too. The plan was meant to work from a
closer range than this. Ostentatiously,Craven signals:
Harris moves out yet again. And he moves a third
time. Trevathan finds the evidence of his eyes a little
hard to credit. What manner of dive pass is this to be?
But Harris is his man and he moves out so that he may

cover. The essential first half of the plan has worked. The gap is there.

On the blind side, Craven puts in the ball. Lotz heels like an automaton, Craven has it again – and Turner, with the precision of a stop-watch, streaks through from the blind side wing and has the ball from Craven. Into the gap he sprints, the gap where Trevathan was, but is not . . .and on, bearing infield with the defence completely out of the picture and up to Taylor, with Lochner, Babrow and Williams racing up to link with him.

If they had drilled the move a dozen years, these Springboks, they might have bettered it. Turner to Lochner now, Lochner to Babrow – and Babrow, near the córner flag, is over. Eden Park, like the ranks of Tuscany in days of old, can scarce forbear . . .though this is the death-knell for New Zealand, the moment of truth and the tragic dashing of its fondest hopes. But this is vintage Rugby, too, and Eden Park is generous as it roars approval of a brilliant move. Brand is up for the kick, but the target still eludes him. It is 11-3 now, and on the Springbok side is pure and undisguised elation.

Five minutes, and another try. This line is running with the relentless motion of a hard-wound watch. Williams has the ball, beats Mitchell on the outside, then the cover-defence. Now he is up to Taylor, and plunges on. Taylor makes his tackle gamely, but Williams is in full cry and he grasps in vain for a secure grip on those straining thrusting thighs and rolls clear as William bursts across the line and scores. Again no goal. It is 14-3, with another effort yet to come.

Next it was Babrow again, going for the gap and finding it. He ran a shade too far, and Taylor pulled him down. From the ruck came Strachan to secure the ball, fling a long pass to Turner, and see him drive through down the left wing for the fifth and final try.

In a gesture of defiance, Trevathan goaled his second penalty six minutes from the end. Despite the flood of

Springbok scoring, possession had been improved for New Zealand in the second spell when Dalton moved across to the middle of the front row in a desperate effort to improve the heeling. But Sullivan never was brought in to centre, and seldom was there a more conspicuous waste of exceptional talent by a losing side.

The end came with a punted ball rolling for the Springbok line, Williams and "Boy" Louw pursuing it "Let it roll, Dai, and touch it down," called Louw "Time is up". Williams touched down – and the whistle blew.

The praise was unequivocal. The ice was broken, and after three series a rubber had been won and won with clearly-cut decision. Tremendously powerful and specialized forward play, possession from the set scrums where it counted most, superlatively effective half-backs and a three-line which had pace and hands and thrust, these were the attributes of the greatest Springboks.

It was a day on which history was made upon the Rugby field. It was a day, too, when history of a nature far more obvious was being moulded on the Continent: for this was the day of the meeting of Hitler and Mussolini in Munich, a meeting of "heils" and "vivas" and mob hysteria.

Within two years there was war, and for the stalwarts of the great tests of 1937 there were sterner, bitter days ahead. Craven, studying in Germany, escaped through Scandinavia one jump ahead of the jackboots and made his way home to play a notable role with a training battallion. New Zealanders and Springboks were drafted to the Northern battlefields. Cobden, the All Black winger of the opening test, was killed while flying with the R.A.F. Lyster went on to win an M.C. in the desert. Nel, "Boy" Louw, Turner, Bester, Bastard, Babrow and more of them met up again with their erstwhile opponents, Sullivan, Lambourn and others, in North Africa and in Italy. Tony Harris was shot down in action, but survived. Williams, Jennings, Lawton, Martin, Watt and White were all in the thick of it.

It was 12 years before the great matches were resumed, and a new generation was left to revive the memories of this day of days in Auckland, September 25.

THE TEAMS

South Africa: G.H. Brand; F.G. Turner, G.P. Lochner, L. Babrow, D.O. Williams; T.A. Harris, D.H. Craven; M.M. Louw, J.W. Lotz, S.C. Louw, L.C. Strachan, M.A. van den Berg, P.J. Nel *(capt.)*, W.E. Bastard and W.F. Bergh.

New Zealand: J.M. Taylor; T.H.C. Caughey, N.A. Mitchell, J.L. Sullivan; J.A. Hooper, D. Trevathan; H.J. Simon; E.S. Jackson, A. Lambourn, D. Dalton, R.M. McKenzie, R.R. King *(capt.)*, S.T. Reid, R.H. Ward and A.A. Parkhill.

Referee: Mr. J.S. King.

South Africa – five tries (Babrow 2, Bergh, Turner, Williams), one conversion (Brand), 17 points.

New Zealand – two penalty goals (Trevathan), 6 points.

They came back to South Africa as heroes, the team a newsman dubbed the "best team ever to leave New Zealand". Many had become household names, and many of them were backs as South Africa discovered again its ability to run with the ball in the post-Osler era. And one of them was the new fly half Tony Harris, as talented a sportsman as South Africa has ever produced.

For some it was the end of the road in international rugby. On the voyage Philip Nel dropped his boots overboard, a symbol of his determination not to play again. Others were in action the next year against the Lions, Craven as captain with Boy Louw as his vice-captain.

It was 34 years later that the next team won a series in New Zealand – the 1971 Lions. And the only other team after that was the Wallabies in 1986. Teams don't often win in New Zealand. None has done so as the 1937 Springboks did – five tries to nil in the decider. And yet Danie Craven considers the 1951-2 Springboks in the UK a better side.

Let the skipper, Philip Nel, have the last word. "It has been a privilege and a honour to captain such a team, who not only played football in the best traditions of the game but

57

also proved that bright football was not necessarily losing football."

Tour Record:	P	W	D	L	Pf	Pa
In Australia	11	10	-	1	444	76
In New Zealand	17	16	-	1	411	104
Tests:						
vs Australia	2	2	-	-	35	22
vs New Zealand	3	2	-	1	37	25

When the *Rugby Almanack* of New Zealand celebrated its golden jubilee it picked its best team from players who had visited New Zealand during that time. Gerry Brand was at fullback, Danie Craven at scrum half, and Jan Lotz at hooker. Freddie Turner was a reserve.

BOBBY AND THE BRITISH OPEN

Portly, placid, and plus-foured as he is probably remembered, it's hard to think of Bobby Locke as a child prodigy, and yet he was in a way that Gary Player was not. Somehow Bobby Locke always seemed middle-aged. Even his real names – Arthur D'Arcy – seemed to belong to a different era. He was in fact given his nickname not from Bobby Jones, the great golfer, but by a servant who could not cope with his given names and produced something that sounded vaguely like Bobby.

Locke started at four with a cut-down club, was a member of Germiston Golf Club at six, won his first trophy at thirteen when his handicap was 12, and became the youngest golfer to win the double – the South African Amateur and the S.A. Open. That was in 1935, the year Gary Player was born.

As Locke said, "Golf was my best subject at school. For years I persevered at golf when my schoolboy friends were going off to play football."

In 1937 he was awarded his Springbok blazer for a tour of Britain, before turning professional in 1938, at the age of 20. In that year he won the South African, New Zealand, and Irish Opens. Later he would win the Mexican, Dutch, French, Egyptian, German, Australian and Canadian Opens, apart from more pretigious tournaments in Britain and the USA.

In six years starting 1935 he won the S.A. Open five times and then went off to the North African desert with the South African Air Force. In 1946 he won the first S.A. Open after the War. In all he won it nine times.

In 1947 and 1948 he campaigned in America, and the Yanks did not like him. In fact they so disliked him that they did not want to let him back. They called him names, like Poker-faced Puttin' Pete. In truth the Americans did not like

Locke because he took so much of their money.

The British public were fonder of him – after all a South African in those days was at least part Brit, especially if his names were Arthur D'Arcy Locke.

In 1946 Bobby Locke, with his black cat and silver horseshoe for luck, played the British Open, which Sam Snead won with Locke runner-up.

Bobby Locke came back to Britain from the USA at the end of June 1949, with the British Open due to start at Royal St George's course at Sandwich in Kent. It was not a happy arrival. Appendicitis was threatening, and his American adventure had been less successful than he had promised when he left Palmietfontein for the USA. Furthermore Bobby Locke had not got on all that well with British golfers up till then. But things soon fell into place.

His practice rounds went well despite a smaller ball than the one used in the USA, and Ludbrokes quoted him at 6 to 1, top of the betting. Locke, immaculate in dress and manner, called by *The Observer* "the natural successor to Hagen as the Beau Brummel of the links", captured the imagination, and crowds came to golf for the first time. The course, in fact, was not to have another Brittish Open for 32 years, because of its inability to cope with crowds. And the crowd had its own money's worth of excitement.

The year, 1949, was an interesting one for South Africans. Apartheid was settling in with, amongst other things, a bill before parliament to forbid mixed marriages, Milne and Erleigh were up for trial for fiddles, Robey Leibbrandt was on trial, a lady called Ruth Williams had met a man called Seretse Kama, and Ebbo Bastard, the 1937 rugby Springbok, was shot dead.

Sport was interesting during that South African winter. Milesia Pride won the Durban July, Eric Sturgess and Sheila Summers won Wimbledon, Len Hutton was breaking records in England, and – glory of glories – the All Blacks were touring South Africa. The All Blacks lost 6-5 to Eastern Transvaal on the day the Durbun July was run, two days before the opening round of the British Open at Royal Cinque Ports Course at Deal, the last time the British Open was played there, and now, so it seems, off the Open roster forever. In 1949 salt seas burnt the grass and the Open was moved down to Sandwich.

Locke's first competition round in Britain had been at Addington Palace Country Club near Croydon where he broke a 15-year-old record by going round in 10 under par. The day before the Open he relaxed, yachting.

The first qualifying round saw Bobby Locke off to a good start. He had the honour of driving off the first ball and got a birdie three at first hole of the difficult course. His went round in 69, and the second day was at Sandwich, the Royal St George's Course.

Of the 230 players entered for the Open 96 qualified – amongst them eight amateurs – for the first round proper on Wednesday, 6th July, 1949, with the main challenge for Locke likely to come from Johnny Bulla of the USA and Ken Bousfield.

The day was warm, the course pleasant, and Bobby Locke of South Africa started well – out in 32. Then came the 14th, called Suez Canal where the drive carries over sandhills with the canal some 300 yards from the tee of this 520-yard hole. It is the most difficult hole on the course, and Bobby Locke drove out of bounds to the right and ended with a seven. His 69 for the first round put him two behind James Adams of Scotland and one behind Harry Bradshaw from Kilcroney in Ireland, a natural golfer who played badly and quickly while Locke was deliberate. Ken Bousfield was also on 69.

The 14th had an obvious effect on Locke. He had been six under par until then. He cut his drive, incurred a penalty stroke, and, according to F.C.W. Pignon the golf critic, "we saw a very different Locke. He was just an ordinary golfer, and a very ordinary one at that."

Bradshaw had not had the luck of the Irish. It's bad enough to get into the rough but a lot worse to end up at the bottom of a broken beer bottle. His niblick sent glass flying but popped the ball out only a few yards. The broken beer bottle cost him a shot. Bobby Locke had reason to be grateful to the beer bottle.

The second round was played in cold weather with a

61

strong wind from the north west. Cold hands, rotten luck, a troublesome putter ("I just could not get into my stride. I played badly and did not have any idea on the green") were countered by icy determination, and his 76 pulled him one back on Bradshaw and Adams who had both had a 77, but in the meantime Max Faulkner had swept into the lead with a 71 for 142, followed by Frank Stranahan of the USA on 144. Late in the day came the biggest surprise; the leader was Sam King of the UK on 140. Bobby Locke was five behind the leader.

At the end of the second day Locke said, "When I missed the short putt at the third I seemed to lose all confidence in my game, especially on the greens. I certainly did not play well." But the imperturbable features showed nothing and on the third day, in the cold, Locke's putter was hot again.

The skies were grey, the weather cold, and Locke shot a 68 with a magnificent outward half. Bradshaw also had a 68, and, going into the last day, these two and Faulkner shared the lead.

The last round yoyoed for Locke. He was in control, he cracked, and then he come back miraculously, and still it was not enough. Bradshaw finished on 70, and there were several who thought that he had won, though the likeable Irishman slipped away for the long tense wait while Locke played. "One never knows with Locke," Bradshaw said.

The first nine were fine – 32, which was what Bradshaw had done. Then he dropped a shot on the tenth when he three-putted. The sixteenth, the best of the short holes at 165 yards, has eight bunkers. In 1967 Tony Jacklin holed in one in the Dunlop Masters. Bobby Locke was one over par with a four.

Two holes to play. Locke needed a three and a four to tie. The seventeeth is a humpy 423 yards. The last hole is 441 yards, and has decided many championships as it is easy to miss the green. Both holes are par fours. Locke needed a birdie to tie. Locke decided that while there was life, there was hope.

His drive was long and to the right of the fairway. He marched after the ball while a crowd of several thousand scrambled after him. The next shot was the one that mattered, and everybody knew that. Bobby Locke produced a shot in a million.

He inspected the whole area from ball to hole, selected a six iron, and pitched the ball high and straight to stop 5 yards from the flag. It was the most valuable shot of the whole championship. Locke holed the putt. He had his birdie. But there was still the 18th to play.

He drove straight down the fairway but halted his second shot to ask a fan with a movie camera to stop because the whirring sound was putting him off. It was a tense moment. His iron shot was just a few inches short of the top of the green, 20 yards from the pin. The crowd held its breath as he putted and cheered when his putt stopped just 2 feet beyond the hole. In fact he did not hole a single long putt in the Open.

Locke took a long time over the last putt, but down it went, and he had tied with Bradshaw, the seventh tie in the history of the British Open up till then. Now for the 36 hole play – off but first Bradshaw and Locke had a beer together. After all, with 283, they had equalled the championship record.

The betting on Locke shortened to 6 to 4 on.

The first four holes were level and then at the fifth, Bradshaw missed a putt from four feet. At the seventh he dropped another shot, when Locke played a magnificent brassie second into the teeth of the wind.

Par	5	4	4	5	3	5	3	3	4	= 38
Locke	4	4	3	4	4	3	4	3	4	= 33
Bradshaw	4	4	3	4	5	3	5	3	4	= 35

On the way back the tenth and eleventh were shared but Bradshaw dropped another shot on the 12th, again missing a short putt. Then came Suez Canal. Locke's second shot stopped two feet from the pin, Bradshaw's in a bunker. He struggled to get out and took six for the hole to Locke's eagle three, sweet revenge for the hole's early treatment of him. It killed Bradshaw's chances for he took a six to go six behind.

Bradshaw ended with 74, Locke with 67. Locke, golf's automaton, did not drop a shot in his best round of the tournament.

Par	4	4	4	5	5	5	3	5	5	= 40
Locke	4	4	4	4	3	4	3	4	4	= 34
Bradshaw	4	4	5	4	6	4	3	3	4	= 39

Lunch was taken and the second round got under way. Locke went on his machine-like way and ended the first nine three ahead of Bradshaw. Locke dropped a shot at the 15th, birdied the 17th and won by twelve shots.

Wearing his 1937 Springbok blazer, Bobby Locke accepted the British Open trophy, declaring it "the happiest day in my life!". His father, Mr. C.J. Locke, said, "I was doubtful and thought his early score of 76 a bad sign, but mother has been quite certain all along that Bobby would win. We are now very relieved."

The press had many glorious things to say, including suggesting that Bobby Locke was the best golfer in the world. *The Times* (the London newspaper) said, "All his cares had dropped from him and he was at his serenest, inexorable best." *The Manchester Guardian* said, "His last two rounds on Saturday put his golfing supremacy almost beyond question for there is probably no player in the world, even coming fresh to the game, who would have stood up to Locke's figures."

As a tailpiece, F.C.J. Pignon reckoned that winning the Open would be worth all of £10 000 to Locke. Money had a different value then. The prize money for winning the Open was £300.

Just for the record the leading scores were:

285 Robert de Vicenzo (Argentina)
286 Sam King, Charles Ward
287 Max Faulkner, Arthur Lees
288 James Adams, Wally Smithers, Johnny Fallon
289 Ken Bousfield, Bill Shankland
290 Frank Stranahan, the leading amateur.

Locke said that winning the Open and taking the cup back

to South Africa for the first time was his greatest ambition. "I shall take great care of it and I promise to bring it back with me next year."

Bobby Locke won the British Open the next year and again in 1952 and 1957. He was probably the best golfer in the world at the time, vastly popular, determined, well mannered, and good humoured. The American P.G.A. may not have liked him but the spectators certainly did, and they enjoyed his humour.

When told in the USA that his drives were not long enough, Locke, said, "You drive for show. I putt for dough." And when they told him that he had a weak left hand, he said, "Don't worry about that – I take all my cheques with my right hand."

In the USA Locke had learned to use a wedge, an American invention, and this had improved his approach shots. The USA had also forced him to learn to get out of a bunker accurately. "You must get down in two from a trap if you are going to win." In the play-off with Bradshaw Locke was only once in a bunker and he got out well enough to hole the putt.

Locke made you proud to be a South African – and also took your mind off the All Black defeat of Western Province, a defeat that forced the selectors to rethink their team for the first test since before the war.

Nice guys can come first.

WIMBLEDON TRIUMPH

In no other sport have South Africans disappointed as regularly as in tennis. Think of them – Kevin Curren in the Wimbledon final, Johan Kriek, Sandra Reynolds, Ross Fairbanks. It goes even further. In 1921 Brian Norton reached the finals of the men's singles and won the first two sets against Big Bill Tilden, threw away the next two, had match point in the fifth and lost. It was possibly the luckiest win of Tilden's long career.

There were some successes. Charlie Winslow in 1912 and Louis Raymond in 1920 won the singles at the Olympic Games. Just to keep it in perspective the USA won the gold medal for rugby at the Olympics about this time, too. In 1928 PDB Spence of South Africa partnered Elizabeth Ryan of the USA to win the mixed doubles at Wimbledon.

1949 was South Africa's best year at Wimbledon. The star was Eric Sturgess, and they don't come nicer than Eric William Sturgess, as Dick Stent's story records:

> The story goes that a prospective pilot was being interviewed about his aptitude for flying by Air Force authorities just after the outbreak of the Second World War and the conversation went along these lines –
> Air Force Officer: Do you play any games?
> Prospective Pilot: Well, yes.
> A.F.O.: What games do you play?
> P.P.: Well, I've played cricket.
> A.F.O.: Have you been in any teams?
> P.P.: Some school teams.
> A.F.O.: Um, ah. Do you play anything else besides cricket?
> P.P.: Well, I play tennis.
> A.F.O.: Tennis, eh? Played any tournament tennis?

P.P.: A little.

A.F.O.: Ever won anything?

P.P.: Well, I won my club tournament.

A.F.O.: Nothing better than that?

P.P.: Well, I won the provincial tournament, too.

A.F.O.: You did, eh? I don't suppose you won the South African championship, too?

P.P.: Well, as a matter of fact, I did.

A.F.O.: Look here, what did you say your name was?

P.P.: Eric Sturgess.

The story may be apocryphal but it is typical of the ultramodest Sturgess. Quietly-spoken and self-effacing to a degree, Sturgess is completely unaffected by the many successes that have come his way in tennis world.

While one cannot think of Sturgess and the word "ambition" in the same breath, it is obvious that he must, a long time ago, have set his heart on winning the men's singles title at Wimbledon.

Several good cricket judges have said that, had Sturgess not decided to make tennis his main interest, he would have played cricket for South Africa. During the war, indeed, there were so many good cricketers in the services that a match was organised between them and the Rest of South Africa. The Services side, captained by Hammond, contained only one player who was not an international – that is, a cricket international – and it was Sturgess.

Sturgess first won the South African men's singles title at the age of 19, in 1939. He joined the S.A.A.F. next year and had a very good record as a pilot on light bombers. In May 1945, right at the tail end of the war, he was shot down and had to bale out. Like Tony Harris, another great all-rounder, he spent several months in a P.O.W. camp in Germany before he was released by the Russians and sent to England.

He soon picked up the threads after the war and apart from maintaining his hold on the South African championships, Eric often won tournaments in other countries. He became champion of Sweden, of Holland, of Ireland and of the Argentine,among others, and he reached the final of the United States singles in 1948 at Forest Hill, there to be beaten by "Pancho"Gonzales, who afterwards did very well as a professional.

The Americans said that he had the most perfect court manners in the world, and that was in days when nobody would have dreamed of behaving like McEnroe, Kriek, and co. A South African sportswriter said of him in 1954. "Both as a player and as a gentleman he brought more fame to South Africa then any other amateur sportsman in the last 10 years." He played on the centre courts of nineteen different countries without a word of complaint about his behaviour from any quarter.

One wonders how Sturgess, a baseline player with a mediocre first and a poor second service, would have fared today, or indeed how any of his generation would have fared in the age of the wunderkind. But then the whizzkids did not have six years cut out of their careers by going off to fight a war. When Sturgess got overseas he was already a veteran of 27. His six years on the international circuit were beyond today's retirement age.

In 1949 Sturgess reached three semi-finals. Ted Schroeder, who went on to beat Jaroslav Drobny in the final, beat Sturgess 3 sets to 2 in the semi-final after Sturgess was up two sets to one. "I fought as hard as I could, but Schroeder was too good for me.

Quick reflexes, quick thinking and control of the lob made Sturgess an excellent doubles player, and it is here that he achieved success at Wimbledon.

In the men's doubles he and Budge Patty of the USA reach the semi-finals where they lost to the eventual winners Pancho Gonzales and F. Parker of the USA. The score – 6-8, 6-3-7-5, 3-6, 6-3.

Sturgess's partner in the mixed doubles was Mrs Sheila Summers, who, as Sheila Piercey, had gone to England with the 1938 Springbok team. She was then a teenager. Dick Stent continues:

The blonde, slightly-built Sheila was the personification of grace on the court. She was amazingly fast and a stroke player of great grace. Her only fault was that she was inclined to have her on and her off days. This erratic tendency cost her the chance of winning her first South African title in 1946, when Mrs. Mary Muller, whom she had previously beaten five times, blasted her off the court in the final. Most surprisingly, she left all the initiative to Mrs. Muller with sad consequences to herself.

However, Sheila soon proved herself to be on world-class level and, in 1947, in an unofficial world ranking list she was placed as high as No.5. A great victory in the quarter-finals at Wimbledon that year over Mrs. Pat Todd and a good fight against the eventual winner, Miss Margaret Osborne, had earned her this place.

A tour to America in 1948 further matured her game and it was then that she beat Dorothy Head in the Mexican Pan-American championships' women's singles, the score in the final being 11-9, 6-2. Sturgess, who was hailed at this tournament as the "South African Perfectionist", incidentally, had his revenge on Gonzales, who had beaten him a few weeks earlier in the United States championships, winning 11-9, 6-0, 6-4.

Sturgess and Miss Summers were seeded fourth and reached the fourth round with consummate ease, beating Eustace Fannin and his partner *en route*. In the quarter-finals they met Geoff Brown and Joyce Fitch of Australia, who had beaten them in the final of the South African Championships a month or so earlier. The South Africans lost the first set but managed to win the next two to reach the semi-finals where the going was even tougher. They beat O.W. Sidwell of Australia and Mrs. W. du Pont of the USA 6-4, 7-9 (There were no tie-breaks in those days), and 6-3, as the South Africans lobbed back their opponents powerful blasts.

The two Springboks had, as their opponents in the "United" final, the Australian, John Bromwich, and the great American player, Louisa Brough. It was a brilliant, pulsating match, in which the fortunes went first one way, then, dramatically, the other. For a long time Bromwich and Miss Brough directed their fire almost continiously at Mrs. Summers, who returned Bromwich's drives and smashes. And it was she who found a gap between her opponents to enable her side to break through and win the fifteenth game of the first set, taking Miss Brough's service for an 8-7 lead. Sturgess served next and won the game for the set at 9-7.

Bromwich now resorted to lobs to break up the Springbok combination. Sturgess sidestepped from one flank to the other, in a constant interchange of position with Mrs. Summers, and the couples fought neck and neck for the second set. Eventually, this set was lost by the South Africans at 11-9 and the final set started in an atmosphere of tense expectation.

Bromwich's wily game continued to prevent Sturgess from dictating the match as completely as he had done in the semi-final against Sidwell and Mrs. du Pont. But in spite of Bromwich's clever tactics, Sturgess's speed and accomplished stroke play enabled him slightly to outshade the Australian in vigorous smashes and superbly played drives and volleys. Sturgess also now resorted occasionally to the judicious use of lobs to the back of the court. Mrs. Summers, with her racket sometimes gripped hard in both hands, stood up unflinchingly to the fierce shots that her opponents rained on her and she sent most of them back where often Bromwhich or Miss Brough found the net or overdrove in their efforts to keep up the high pace.

Relatively, there was a slight lack of power in Mrs. Summers's service, but this was compensated for by great agility of Sturgess at the net and, conceding only an occasional point himself when he served, the South African champion saw his side level the scores at 5-5. Miss Brough served next and the Springboks made their greatest effort, whipping back everything low and hard first to one corner and then the other, passing

Bromwich at the net and placing the ball between their opponents with consummate skill. They broke through and led 6-5.

Now it was Mrs. Summers's service. Would the others return the compliment? But Sturgess covered everything and smashing with great effect, the game, the set and the match were won.

The usually undemonstrative Sturgess leaped in the air with glee and Mrs. Summers danced delightedly as the crowd rose to give the South African couple a great reception.

Commented the *Cape Times:* Mrs. Sheila Summers and Mr. Eric Sturgess have put a combined feather in the cap of South African sport by their historic victory at Wimbledon. A gruelling and exciting match brought a win on that most famous tennis court in the world which can only be attributed to outstanding skill and outstanding spirit.

"Nothing is lost by South Africans applying a little pat on the back to themselves for the prowess and success of their representatives on this occasion. In quite recent times, our best tennis players were being patted considerately on the shoulder by visiting teams and told, paternally, that although the standard of play lacked the first-class touch, all hopes of future honours should scarcely be abondoned. A future race may arise, as it were!

"It seems to have come pretty quickly. Wits, stamina and spirit were required, in trying circumstances, to carry off the fight. In their triumph, Sturgess and Mrs. Summers have proclaimed to all concerned that South Africa is not so immature in sport as is sometimes suggested."

Sheila Summers did not return to Wimbledon but Eric Sturgess was back again in 1950, knocked out in the quarter-finals of the singles by Vic Seixas, but he and Louise Brough, his opponent in 1949, teamed up to beat Frank Sedgman of Australia and Doris Hart of the USA 6-2, 9-7 in the final.

In 1952 Sturgess again made the semi-final of the singles only to be blasted away by Ken McGregor of Australia. In 1951 and 1952 he was runner-up in the men's doubles, first with Jaroslav Drobny, then with Vic Seixas. But by then he was 32.

Perhaps the greatest victory of the South Africans at Wimbledon in 1949 was just simply the victory of goodness.

THE BOOT STRIKES

There has never, in my experience, been a rugby match like it. Nothing has ever matched the sheer, mad excitement of the first test against the All Blacks in 1949.

I know it was not a marvellously flowing game. I know that it was too controvesial for the game's good. I know that it had an unpleasant aftermath. I know all that, but it still remains in my mind the most thrilling rugby occasion of my life.

It was the first test after the war, after a gap of 11 years. I had never seen a test match, but in those days we believed that the Springboks were the greatest rugby players on earth and that they always won, but that the All Blacks were worthy opponents. And here were the All Blacks. We followed every move of theirs with wonder.

A group came to my school, Marist Brothers in Rondebosch, and planted trees. Dave Stewart's father obtained an All Black jersey. They went off to Hermanus for nearly a month and then kicked off the tour at 3.54 p.m. on Union Day, 31st May, against Southern Universities at Newlands. For a start they threw the ball around and cruised to an 11-0 lead by 18 minutes past four but with twenty minutes to go to fulltime the All Blacks were desperately clinging to a two point lead, which they maintained though there were pictures in the paper proving that Basil Butler had scored a try when he and Peter Henderson dived for the ball that Ralph Burmeister had made a mistake. Of course, to the juvenile mind referees don't make mistakes – they cheat, though it never occurred to us to ask why Ralph Burmeister who lived in Cape Town would have cheated.

The New Zealanders then started their wanderings around the country, never to reproduce the glamour of those first twenty two minutes until the last "match" of the tour, an

Bobby Locke on his way to his British Open triumph in 1949

Sheila Summers (left) and Eric Sturgess won the mixed doubles title at Wimbledon in 1949

Above: Okey Geffin (third from the right) succeeds with his fifth and final penalty in the 1st test against the All Blacks in 1949

Below: Peter Henderson scores the All Black try in the same test. Cecil Moss is too late to stop him

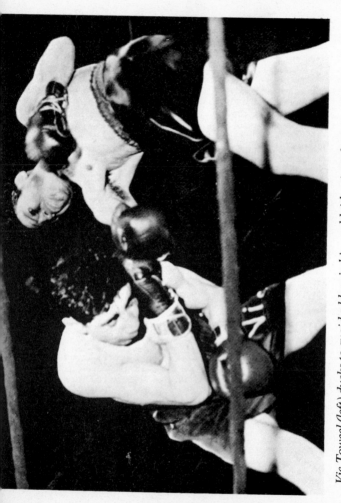

Vic Toweel (left) ducks to avoid a blow in his world title triumph against Manuel Ortiz

additional, unofficial match at Newlands with Town Clubs which resulted in a draw but only after Bob Scott came on as a subsistiute – yes, in those days more than 30 years before the IRB sanctioned subsititution – for Jim Kearney.

Their wanderings included defeat at the hands of Basil Kenyon's Border side, a draw with Orange Free State in Kroonstad, a one-point defeat by Eastern Transvaal but victories over Eastern Province, Transvaal, and then, most significantly, over Western Province.

The margin of victory in the Western Province match was only 6-3, but it had been expected that the home team would beat the All Blacks. The selectors were forced to change their minds.

Selection had run a funny path that year. There had been trials on the go in Pretoria when the All Blacks docked in Cape Town on 5th May, 1949. The All Blacks flew up their assistant manager, Alec McDonald, and their vice-captain, Ray Dalton, Andy's father, to watch the trials when the South African scrummaging and goal kicking caused them to shudder. After the trials the South African selectors announced a short list of 32 players for the first test which was to be played at Newlands on 16th July – two months and a thousand miles away. Of those 32 players eleven played in the first test. Fourteen of the 32 never played for South Africa. The four "outsiders" chosen were Jack van der Schyff, Buks Marais, who was 21, Cecil Moss, and Hansie Brewis. As the series went on they would be joined by others: Ryk van Schoor, Fonnie du Toit, Carrots Geraghty – by which time the only back on the short list actually in the Springbok team was Tjol Lategan – Willem Barnard, Piet Malan, and Salty du Rand.

One player who was always there was Okey Geffin – and not for his kicking. He was chosen as a prop. In fact Geffin was only fourth choice ("as a last resort" as Craven said before the first test) kicker after Jack van der Schyff, Hansie Brewis and Floors Duvenhage. How he got in the act was possibly inspiration, possibly madness, certainly chutzpah.

The selectors, led by Bill Schreiner, sought privacy in the committee room of the Olympic Sports Club in Rondebosch as they hastily reviewed their thoughts of the night before.

They dropped three Western Province players: Dennis Fry, Otto van Niekerk and Chum Ochse. Later, at the dinner given for the All Blacks and the Western Province teams, Bill Schreiner, flanked by his other four selectors, announced the Springbok team to cheers. The All Black team was also announced that night.

For the next week, Bobby Locke and Wimbledon and everything else were forgotten. Nothing but the coming test would absorb our minds.

For the only time since the first test in 1891 the Springboks would feld a team composed entirely of new caps: Jack van der Schyff; Buks Marais, Floors Duvenhage (vice-captain), Tjol Lategan, Cecil Moss; Hansie Brewis, Ballie Wahl; Okey Geffin, Jorrie Jordaan, Hoppy van Jaarsveld; Fiks van der Merwe, Bubbles Koch, Felix du Plessis (captain), Louis Strydom; Hennie Muller. Danie Craven, then in his first year as a national selector, was the manager. After all he was the last man to captain South Africa in a test.

The All Blacks had new caps in Peter Henderson on the wing, Larry Savage at scrum half, the not-yet notorious Kevin Skinner at prop and Lester Harvey at lock. The All Blacks greatest problem on the tour, once Bo Wintle and Danie Craven got their scrumming right, was at half back but then they had been forced to leave behind their best ones, Ben Couch and Vince Bevan, because they were Maoris, and in those days South Africa did not allow Maoris to tour and the New Zealanders acquiesced.

I got to the ground at about three in the morning of 16th July, 1949 and met there my friend, Ronnie Brorson, and we were a long way down the railway line to Rondebosch in the queue that had been there through the night. But long before the gates opened tussling broke out amongst the big lads, and we discovered that little fellows like us could worm our way forward.

When the gates opened at 11 am we were in the forefront and rushed to get seats on the half-way line on the Railway Stand side of the field. For all the early start to the day and its long rigours, at no stage did I feel tired.

What a crush! They closed the gates. People jumped over the old tin fence. Those who could still not see got a ladder and put it up against the old Malay Stand till the police cleared them off the roof. The Springboks on their way to the ground were caught in a traffic jam and actually did much of their changing in the bus. Half-dressed they were hustled into the ground, and down to their changerooms where they finished changing and ran onto the field. There was not much time for talking or getting minds right.

The roaring and excitement and frenzy of 42 000 people as the Springboks ran out onto the field was something I have never since experienced. South Africa kicked off from the town end, the forwards lining up towards the Railway Stand. Suddenly Floors Duvenhage kicked off to the right and Cecil Moss hared after the ball. Eric Boggs got there first but Moss bundled him out. In those days "forced out" was your ball, but the Springboks won the line-out and Brewis sliced a drop at goal which Buks Marais chased but the bounce beat him, and the All Blacks survived. Then Jack van der Schyff had a fairly easy penalty kick, which he missed.

From then on the half belonged to the All Blacks. Jim Kearney and Bob Scott both missed penalty kicks at goal, but the signs were all there as Scott kept driving the Springboks back and Elvidge and Henderson were causing all sorts of problems for Duvenhage and Marais.

After 15 minutes Bob Scott succeeded with a penalty and then – gloom and despondency – Peter Henderson charged down Jack van der Schyff's clearance from the cornerflag on the Grand Stand side and just beat Buks Marais to touch down just inside the dead-ball line. The referee delayed his decision as he checked the spot to make sure it was within Newlands's 25-yard goal area. Scott converted. 19 minutes, and the All Blacks were up 8-0.

After Jack van der Schyff missed another kick at goal, a strange, unplanned occurrence set a hefty prop from the Wanderers club in Johannesburg on the road to fame.

Although New Zealand heeled the ball in the scrum, Lachie Grant was penalised for off-side. As the scrum broke up Okey Geffin, who had practised kicking for so long in a prisoner-of-war camp, found the ball at his feet. He grabbed the ball and placed it, hearing no contradictory order from Felix du Plessis, 10 yards in from touch and 25 yards from the New Zealand goal line. There was only the slightest of breezes into the Springboks' faces.

There was no sand in those days and round-the-corner kickers played soccer. Geffin dug a hole pointing at the middle of the New Zealand crossbar. He dug it with his left foot. Digging pushed up a small mound which he fashioned to received the ball, which lay on it with the lace on the ground.

He put his left foot next to the ball, his right foot behind it. He dropped his chin onto his chest, concentrating on the point of the ball near his foot. Then he moved back five rigid paces. Dirty sweaty shorts were hitched, and Okey Geffin moved forward, head down, and his right foot hit the ball and followed through head high. And, in the words of C.K. Friedlander who was running the radio commentary in the days before television, "the ball goes – OVAH!"

The crowd had cheered when the penalty was awarded. Now they roared.

The half was not yet over. Jack van der Schyff was short with a long penalty and Bob Scott started running. He gave to Fred Allen. Allen gave to Jim Kearney who punted high downfield. Oh horrors, Tjol Lategan, a controversial selection, dropped the ball. It was a scrum just inside the Springboks 25 and slap in front of the posts. The All Blacks put in but Jorrie Jordaan took a tight-head. Ballie Wahl fumbled. Another scrum, again New Zealand ball. This time New Zealand heeled, Savage to Kearney and he dropped succesfully for goal and the half time whistle sounded.

New Zealand were full value for their lead, but in most of their matches up to the first test the All Blacks had proved much better in the first half. In fact in eleven of those matches their opponents had outscored them five times in the second half. Only South Western Districts had had a worse second half than first half against the All Blacks.

Okey Geffin says, "The only thought in our minds during the break was that we were all playing in our first Test, and

South Africa was likely to suffer her biggest defeat in history."

In fact Geffin was to make history.

The Springboks attacked at the start of the half but Bob Scott was too much for them and play stayed in midfield. Then, after a break by Ballie Wahl, referee Eddie Hofmeyr penalised the All Blacks 30 yards out for obstruction by Lachie Grant, who, according to the New Zealand version, was trying "to use his left foot fo kick the ball through his own scrum". Thirty yards out and ten yards in from the Railway Stand touch line, not far from us, Geffin hitched his shorts and plodded forward. "OVAH!" 11-6.

Fifteen minutes into the second half, Bubbles Koch won a line-out, Brewis evaded Thornton and kicked for the corner. Henderson threw in seven yards from the New Zealand corner flag. The All Blacks went off-side and that man Geffin made it 11-9. Now excitement bubbled and shouted and screamed.

For ten minutes play see-sawed. Jack van der Schyff pushed Henderson out at the Springbok corner flag. Fred Allen was wide with a drop, and then Jack van der Schyff kicked the Springboks down towards the All Blacks' 25, where they were forced to defend mightily as the Springbok forwards flung themselves at them and Ballie Wahl exploited the blind side.

Bob Scott failed to find touch. Jack van der Schyff essayed a drop but Fred Allen charged the kick down. In those days there was none of the modern tolerance of a charged down kick. If it came off hands or arms it was a knock. Scrum – South Africa's ball. The All Blacks heeled and then came the penalty. Winston McCarthy, who had so many bitter things to say about South African rugby and refereeing after the tour, says that two South African forwards were off-side at the scrum and that Eddie Hofmeyr "first of all decided that Thornton had returned the ball to the scrum, and later decided that Savage had handled the ball in the scrum".

Thirty five yards out it was an not far infield from the Grand Stand touch line, but battle-stained Geffin slotted the kick. 12-11, with eight minutes to play.

Pandemonium. We shouted, we jumped, we threw whatever was loose into the air – hats, coats, lunch boxes, arms. A policeman hurled his helmet into the air and did a somersault on the touch line. The roaring went on and on as Kearney kicked off again.

Soon there was silence as Bob Scott kicked at goal after Hennie Muller was penalised for not playing the ball with the foot after a tackle, as the law then required. But Scott hooked it.

The All Blacks threw the ball around, the Springboks scampered in defence. A loose pass, and Moss footed the ball through and pursued it. Eric Boggs obstructed. Eddie Hofmeyer penalised. Geffin goaled to make it five out of five, a world record broken by Don Clarke when he kicked six penalties to give the All Blacks an 18-17 win over the Lions in 1958 and there were no moans or groans from the All Blacks ("We won within the framework of the rules").

Floors Duvenhage was brought down just short of the New Zealand line and Scott clared for touch. Buks Marais was ready to throw in when Eddie Hofmeyr blew the final whistle.

My mother had given me a small suitcase of food. I threw it into the air and charged across the field with every other urchin at Newlands that day, hearts full of bursting pride. I got caught up in a maelstrom of bodies and, feet only occasionally touching the ground, body twisted, I had the pride of having Felix du Plessis's backside on my neck as the crowd carried him off the field.

We milled around in delirium. When I eventually made my ragged way back to the Railway Stand side, Ronnie Brorson was waiting for me with my small suitcase which he had retrieved. Home we went in trains jam-packed with people in an ecstacy that would never die.

Danie Craven would write later, "It was certainly hard on the All Blacks losing like that." To us it did not matter. The Springboks had won; all was right with the world.

In fact the All Blacks, on the only occasion in their history, lost four of the tests on that tour. And they went home to wait for retribution. It came and it was nasty when they won the 1956 series, and the referees struck back first and Kevin

Skinner followed hard. But Craven, again the Springbok manager, said to New Zealand at Eden Park when they made sure of the rubber, "It's all yours, New Zealand."

Back in 1949, we idolised Okey Geffin. They called him The Boot. There were pictures in newspapers with his foot circled. There were pictures of his boot. There were stories of how many pints of milk he drank a day, and suddenly South Africa's youth took to milk. Claude King, the New Zealand newspaper man, even suggested that South Africa erect a statue to Geffin – long before somebody suggested something similar for Naas Botha.

Controversial or not, undeserved victory or not, dull match or not, it remains for me the most exciting rugby match I have ever seen.

There were jokes:

Q.: Did the Springboks win?

A.: Geffinitely.

TOWEEL VS. ORTIZ

Viccie Toweel made you proud, and it was a proud time for South Africans in those years after the War when the full horror of apartheid had not yet been realised.

In those days the Springboks smashed the All Blacks, the best of Europe and the Wallabies; Esther Brand, Joan Harrison, Gerald Dreyer, and George Hunter all won gold medals at the Olympics; Bobby Locke was the greatest golfer in the world; Jack Cheetham's Springboks, against all the odds, had shared the series in Australia; and we had done our bit to squash the evil forces of Nazism and Fascism; the Royal family visited; and Viccie Toweel was the champion of the world.

There were no qualifications to Viccie Toweel's championship. He wasn't the WBC Champion of the World or the WBA Champion of the World. He was simply the Champion of the World, South Africa's first, the poor boy who made good, a figther who was a nice guy.

Boxing's big day in this saga of triumph was 31st May, 1950 – Union Day as it was then called. The hero that day was Viccie Toweel – an unfashionable Lebanese from an unfashionable part of an unfashionable town. From the time he made the sign of the cross to start the first round till referee, Willie Corner, raised his gloved hand in victory, the whole country held its breath. And when the glove went up the country cheered. They loved Viccie Toweel. He made them proud.

But let Chris Greyvenstein tell the Toweel tale as he did in *The Fighters:*

> It was a few days before Christmas 1950. The stoop-shouldered lady, dressed in traditional Lebanese costume of black dress and veil, sat in her favourite wooden

rocking chair. One hand clasped a rosary; the other fingered the *Ring* magazine world championship belt lying in her lap.

There was a smile on her worn face. She never did like her menfolk's love for fighting with their fists, but she understood that this was no common prize. Perhaps she realised that her grandson, Victor Anthony, had won for her family the key to a better life, to full acceptance, in the country she had adopted as a young woman.

She had come to South Africa from Sybil, in the cedar-covered mountains of Lebanon, after the death of her first husband, married here for the second time, and later she and her six-year old son, Michael, had earned their keep by peddling clothes and boot-laces, often beginning their rounds before sunrise to catch the miners on their way to work.

She had watched her son grow to manhood and an existence as hard as the one she had known all her life, had hated and feared his success in the sport of boxing, and when he was still under her control she had refused him permission to compete in a tournament which could have led to selection as a member of the South African team for the Olympic Games in Paris in 1924. The thought of her son going to what she had heard was the pleasure capital of Europe was too much for this devout lady.

The poor eye-sight which in those early days had been enough to keep him out of school also prevented squat and powerful Michael Toweel from making the professional ring his livelihood, which pleased his mother. She was even more pleased when at the age of 19 he married Diana Farah, a Lebanese girl, who like himself had been born in the new country.

She had welcomed the arrival of her grand-children. Jimmy in 1926, Victor in 1928, Maurice in 1930, Alan in 1931, Willie in 1934, Fraser in 1936 and Maureen in 1939. She had watched her son eke out a living for his family in unskilled and often humiliating work and had prayed for him to Our Lady whenever he made his inarticulate protests against fate with a Friday night binge and brawl in the nearby Imperial Hotel.

She had noticed with approval that her son and his wife were bringing up their children in strict accordance with the rules and traditions of the Catholic Church, and were providing a meagre but loving home for their brood, but she had looked on with no sympathy as he taught his boys to fight with their fists. She had been with them when it became clear that the wrong diagnosis had condemned her grandson Maurice to a life of pain as a cripple and she had also suffered during the subsequent years of misery until the boy's courage had showed them that he was to be no burden on his family; that he was as able as any of them to meet the challenges of maturity.

When Jimmy and later, Viccie, fought their way into the newspaper headlines she had listened eagerly to the family discussing their triumphs, her health too feeble to consider attending their bouts. She was as thrilled as any of them when she was told that Vic had won a world title; proud when he had come to see her afterwards with the bruises of battle still on his face.

But it was only now, months after the great occasion, touching the metal and silk of the championship belt, that she fully understood the implications of his feat to her family. Granny Toweel died a few months later, secure in the knowledge that her grandson was the best at his weight in the world and that no-one dared to call them "dirty Syrians" any more.

Perhaps no family in all the history of world boxing can match Pappa Mike's boys. A world title, a draw in a world championship bout, two British Empire titles and seven national championships between Jimmy, Vic and Willie and add to that the fact that Maurice became an internationally-known promotor of world championship fights and that Alan gained an equal measure of fame as a trainer and manager of world title challengers. There were many amateur titles, too, and Vic and

Willie represented their country at the Olympic Games.

For years the corrugated-iron construction with its rough-hewn ring in the back yard of the Toweel home at 12 Balfour Avenue, Benoni, was the most important building in South African boxing. Hot and stuffy when packed far beyond its capacity during the exciting championship years, this was where Pappa taught and trained his sons.

Victor Anthony Toweel, born on January 12, 1928, turned professional nine days after his 21st birhday and 17 months and 14 bouts later he was the bantamweight champion of the world; the first South African to be universally acclaimed as the best in his weight division. As this is written, Vic Toweel is still the only South African to receive general recognition as world champion.

Vic Toweel began his competitive career at the age of nine and he lost only two out of 300 amateur fights. Of his 190 bouts as a senior amateur, Toweel won 160 by knockouts. And yet, in spite of his phenomenal record Toweel was eliminated in the first round of competition at the 1948 Olympic Games in London. He had gone into the ring against Pares of Argentina, suffering from a nose injury sustained in sparring against the Finnish professional Elis Ask, and was judged to have lost on points. The decision was severely criticised by ringside reporters and authorities.

As a professional his career was comparatively brief. He had only 32 fights over a period of five years, winning 28, 14 inside the distance, and being held to a draw once. His three defeats and the draw came after 25 consecutive victories, and in his final year of competition before retiring at the age of 26.

Short and stocky but with slender legs, Vic Toweel was an instinctive boxer-fighter. He could stum up an opponent quickly and intuitively, and he could adapt to any style. He was tough and fearless and until drastic weight reduction and eye trouble took their toll, his stamina was unlimited. At his peak he could hurl punches at an amazing rate and yet his two-fisted attacks were always part of a systematic plan and not the wild, windmill onslaughts of lesser fighters. He was not a heavy puncher but he could hit with authority and the strongest opponents could not afford to take liberties against him.

Taking into account the imponderable contributions of opportunity, character and dedication, Vic Toweel was probably the best-equipped South African fighter of all time; he was certainly invincible between August 6, 1949, when he won his second national title, and November 17, 1951, when he beat Luis Romero in his second world championship defence. Every overseas authority who saw him in action during this period rated him among the best bantamweights in history.

He was a quiet, courteous and dignified champion and has retained these qualities to this day. The ballyhoo of the ring he found repugnant and there was a time during his championship reign when he had his work cut out to hide his dislike of professional boxing. Unlike all the other members of his family, Vic played no role in the business after his own active days were over.

The turning point in his career came when Ronnie Clayton, the British Empire featherweight champion, refused to defend his title against him in 1949. Instead, Stan Rowan, the bantamweight champion, accepted the offer and Toweel had to settle for a future in this division. As a featherweight he would not have had the long, cruel and eventually fatal, battle with the scales, and at the heavier mark he certainly had the strength and ability to have held his own even against such legendary fighters as Willie Pep and Sandy Saddler.

His weight problems began early in his career. After beating Rowan for the Empire bantamweight title he was matched against Jackie Paterson, the former world flyweight champion, and on the morning of the fight he was found to be nearly a kilo over the limit. A harsh laxative, steambaths and rub-downs were needed before he could beat the scales. Negotiations were then already under way for a world title fight with Manuel Ortiz and he had to remain in the bantamweight division or forsake an opportunity which rarely came the way of a South African in those days.

His weight used to rocket to 10 kilograms over the bantamweight limit between bouts and before some of his championship fights he was subjected to dangerous dehydration and pretty near starvation diets. He had to do his roadwork in the heat of the day and much of his sparring, often 16 rounds without a break between, wearing double-thick tracksuits made of woollen blankets. Incalculable harm was done to his system and must account for the abrupt crumbling of his powers when still only 25 years old.

Vic Toweel made his first appearance in the paid ranks on January 21, 1949. Three months later he won the South African bantamweight title when the veteran Jimmy Webster found no other solution but persistent clinching.

It was after this fight that Reg Haswell came into his life. Haswell and his White City Sporting Club had won their rivalry against the antiquated Transvaal National Sporting Club and the former Londoner had inherited Tiny Dean's mantle as the shrewdest and best-connected matchmaker in the country. He had kept an eye on little Viccie ever since he saw him demolish an opponent at the age of 11 and never made any secret of his opinion that he was South Africa's best bet for international honours.

He obtained exclusive rights to the dynamic youngster's services and mapped out a breathtakingly ambitious programme. Toweel beat Jackie Johnson (twice), the veteran John Holt and Plasie Fourie in quick succession, earning little but effectively marking time while Haswell schemed the future. For knocking out Johnson in Springs, Vic was paid in the region of R7 but Pappa Mike, always happier in the gym than hassling with contracts, was confident that the break-through to big money was around the corner. His confidence in Haswell's hustling and his son's ability to beat anybody was to prove justified.

Stan Rowan, of Liverpool, the British and Empire bantamweight champion, was Haswell's target. It seemed risky to give Toweel such an opponent in only his 11th professional fight but it was, in fact, shrewd matchmaking. Rowan, in spite of the titles he had won by beating Jackie Paterson, the former world fly-weight champion earlier in the year, had been showing signs of slipping. He could not cope with the young South African's presistence and fury and at the end of the 15th round he wearily acknowleged his opponent's superiority before the official verdict was announced. Back home a few hours later Vic, completely unmarked, gave an energetic exhibition of jiving with his sister Maureen as his partner.

Toweel was now his country's biggest drawcard; the first bantamweight since the heyday of Willie Smith to capture the public imagination. But while the newspapers speculated about plans for a world title fight the Toweel family nursed a closely-kept secret. Ever since he sparred with Elis Ask in preparation for the London Olympics, Vic had been troubled by a nose injury. It had now reached a point where it was seriously affecting his breathing. Doctors advised an operation but with his next fight already arranged against Jackie Paterson, Scotland's former world flyweight champion, the Toweel's had no option but to wait and hope for the best.

A week before the fight the news leaked out and Paterson immediately offered to do the operation during the fight with his gloves. It was no laughing matter for the Toweels. They knew how much of a handicap Vic really would have to carry into the ring. He solved his problems on his own, as usual. Throwing caution overboard, he attacked from the first bell and for 10 rounds he chased Paterson around the ring, dropping him several times, and winning the easiest of decisions.

In later years Paterson settled in South Africa and he died tragically in 1966 after being stabbed in a night-club brawl.

The operation to his nose was a success but it knocked him out of action for two months while Haswell became locked in battle with Jack Solomons, then Britain's premier promoter, over the services of Manuel Ortiz, the world bantamweight champion. Solomons wanted Ortiz to defend his title against Danny O'Sullivan in London and for a while it looked as if his superior resources would prevail.

Haswell did the sensible thing by sending a represent-ative to California to negotiate personally with the champion, however, and after weeks of wrangling, Ortiz's signature was secured.

Ortiz was one of boxing's great champions and the job of beating him must have worried a 22-year-old challenger in his 16th month as a professional and with only 13 bouts to his credit. But if Vic Toweel had doubts in the deep confines of his mind, his dark, mournful eyes never gave him away. He freely acknow-ledged his respect for the world champion but claimed in that quiet voice of his that he looked on it as just another fight. For the first time in his career he did not do his preparations in the old backyard shack.

He trained at Clonmell Kennels, promoter Haswell's sprawling estate near Alberton. There he lived in a truly Spartan manner, doing miles and miles of road-work every morning, dressed in a special track suit made from thick Basuto blankets with, more often than not, layers of inner-tubing wrapped tightly round his hips and torso to help melt away the excess weight.

Teams of sparring partners wilted before his fury. His reflexes were honed to such a degree of sharpness that it sometimes appeared as if the pear-shaped punch-bag was tied to his gloves with invisible threads. Such was the consummate ease with which he handled that devilishly unpredictable contraption.

And always there was the close watch on food and

liquid. Weak tea, dry toast, poached eggs, steak and salads. That was all he could have – and not a lot of it, either.

In the meantime his famous opponent had arrived in Johannesburg in a blaze of publicity.

Manual Ortiz was then 33 and a veteran of twelve years in the prize-ring. He had first won the title eight years before, and then defended it successfully 15 times before losing it to Harold Dade. Three months later he had regained it. The fight against Toweel was to be the fourth defence of his second reign.

Ortiz was a stockily-built Mexican-American with a skin the colour of polished oak. Colourful ties were then the fashion, and Ortiz had a collection which virtually screamed across a room. His young, plump and equally dark-skinned trainer, Ray Luna, did most of the talking for the champion, a man who was not much of a conversationalist.

One afternoon, after a long run over a nearby golf course, Ortiz asked me if Toweel was a "hit-and-run" type of fighter. When I assured him that our champion was still to take his first retreating step in the professional ring, Ortiz seemed relieved.

"Then I will take him," he said confidently. "My legs are shot and I can no longer catch the runners. If he comes to me I will have no trouble."

In his training, Ortiz looked every inch the champion. The American concert pianist Jose Iturbi was visiting Johannesburg, and he was so interested in the welfare of his countryman that he virtually became Ortiz's assistant trainer. He never missed a session in the gym and he often acted as a spokesman for the champion.

Toweel and Ortiz met once or twice for publicity purposes, and I noticed that they seemed to have an instinctive liking for one another. On the Sunday before the fight – postponements pushed the date back to Wednesday, May 31 – champion and challenger attended Mass in the same church. Ortiz was rather late and the church full, and so it happened that he took a seat next to Vic's younger brother Willie, himself destined to become a champion a few years later.

During the service, Ortiz turned to him and whispered. "I wonder whose prayers are going to be answered?"

He merely smiled when Willy loyally replied that Vic, being the better fighter, would surely be allowed to win!

Two weeks before the fight, Vic began, literally, to get cold feet. It is a strange fact that Vic Toweel always suffered from cold feet when a big fight was drawing near. Sometimes it became so bad that three or four blankets had to be stacked over his feet before he felt comfortable enough to sleep. If this phenomenon was due to his nerves, it was certainly the only way that they affected him. He had an abnormally slow pulse beat of just over 40, which was said to account for his exceptional stamina.

Like many other great fighters, Vic was also inclined to be sullen and sulky for the last few days before the fight. He was invariably co-operative with photographers and reporters, but you could feel the controlled resentment and truculence raging inside him.

The night before the fight, Vic left his training camp to spend the last hours at the Toweel home at 12, Balfour Avenue, Benoni. He was in magnificent condition except for a painful ear and nose, the result of blows received in sparring. His family were frantically worried about this, but Vic insisted that it did not bother him in the least.

At nine o'clock he went to sleep in a single bed in the room of his brother Maurice.

Maurice had the saving grace of sleeping best when most deeply worried, and the family thought he was least likely to keep Vic awake by constantly tossing and turning.

"As far as we know, my brother slept like a top that night," Maurice once told me. "We both woke up very early, and Vic's blankets and sheets were all perfectly straight, as if the bed had just been made. Willie used to wrestle the sheets constantly before a big fight, but Vic always slept without turning over often or violently."

At 6.30 a.m. Vic went to St. Patrick's Church, where Father Conway, an old friend of the family, said Mass.

Once home, he glanced at the newspapers plastered with pictures of himself and Ortiz. Outside the house little groups of people stood talking and hoping for a glimpse of the challenger.

At the weigh-in, both champion and challenger were well within the bantamweight limit, but Vic at any rate had had to forego liquids for many hours in order to manage it.

The moment he was in the car for the journey back to Benoni, he began to drink bottle after bottle of fizzy, soft drinks. By the time he reached home, he was feeling almost cheerful.

He ate a big steak and then slept right through the afternoon until after five.

When he rose, the family noticed that he was paler than usual. He ate a poached egg and a slice of toast and drank some tea before walking a couple of blocks to his grandfather's house, where he prayed in a private chapel.

Meanwhile his stepmother packed his shorts, socks, boots, groin protector, gum shield and gown. He was to wear velvet trunks with white stripes round the waist and down the sides. On the left leg the word "Vic" was embroided. His stepmother had made the shorts and the gold-coloured gown, decorated with black dragons.

When he returned from the chapel it was time to leave for the arena, as Benoni is 32 km from Johannesburg.

Accompanied by his father, his brother Jimmy, uncle Tony Farah and an American adviser, Bernie Feller, Vic got into a blue 1948 Sudebaker. A relative, Jack Farah, was driving. An escort of police on motor cycles guided them to Wembley Stadium where two dance bands were entertaining the thousands who had taken their places hours before.

He was taken directly to his dressing-room. The fight was not due to start until 9.30 p.m. because of broadcasting arrangements. Most members of his family visited him in his dressing-room, beseeching him to be careful. He kept repeating, "Don't worry, don't worry," and appeared to be the calmest person in the room. Pappa Toweel held a rosary in his hand throughout the long waiting period and never ceased muttering prayers.

When he was finally called to the ring, at 9.15 p.m., he was stripped and ready for action. His seconds were Pappa, Bernie Feller, Tony Farah and Bull Nortman (an old friend of the family whose mother had acted as midwife to all the Toweel children).

More than 20 000 people saw Vic Toweel climb through the ropes to the strains of *Sarie Marais*. A towel was draped over his head, and he was pale and serious. He acknowledged the tumultuous welcome with a slight wave of his taped right hand. At the moment Manuel Ortiz entered the ring as a band played *The Stars and Stripes Forever*. Ortiz wore a drab brown gown with the words "Golden Gloves" embroidered on the back. His trunks were purple with a black stripe.

Vic immediately walked over to shake hands. He admitted afterwards that he felt a pang of fear as he touched Ortiz's knuckles, taped so well that the whole hand had less resilience than a cricket ball.

Referee Willie Corner, whose selection was criticized in some circles on the grounds that he was too old, called the two to the centre of the ring to give them the required instructions. Then they shook hands again and went back to their corner to await the bell.

This was how Toweel described his feelings:

"You often hear people talking about mixed emotions. That night I knew what they meant. I was proud to be the first South African to fight for a world title, but at the same time I was very nervous. After all, I had had only 13 professional fights, and there I was to fight Manuel Ortiz, a 33-year-old veteran with 111 professional fights under his belt.

91

"The bell rang and, taking a deep breath, I walked towards Ortiz and the roaring crowd faded as it always did, and all that's left then are you and the other guy."

"Don't go wild. Find out what he is like. Don't rush," was the last advice his father whispered in his ear.

Now let Vic Toweel tell the story of his 45 minutes of glory:

"For two, three rounds I took it easy. I did this in most of my fights. I liked getting the feel of things before throwing everything into it. I always took a few rounds to study my opponent's style.

"I realized immediately that I was dealing with a man who was cleverer than I, who could hit harder and who was also stronger. My speed was my only trump card and I was also convinced that I could last better. Ortiz was older. I decided to force the pace and not to give him a chance to get set for counter-punches.

"For a couple of rounds everything went fine, and then in the eighth all hell broke loose.

"Ortiz started catching me with his right and the punches felt like bricks thrown in my face. One of those whistling rights landed full on my damaged ear. Pain rippled through my body, and when I brought a glove up to the ear, it felt as if my head had swollen to twice its size. And those bombs kept coming.

"My nose was knocked completely out of shape, my head was singing and I was certainly kept conscious only by the sharp pain in my ear. My only thought was: "I'm chucking this fight." I admit it – I wanted to give up because the pain was just too much.

"Somehow I saw out the round, but when I got to my corner I was a beaten fighter.

"Keep to his left, his right hand is a killer," my father whispered as they tried to revive me. Usually I didn't pay too much attention to advice from my corner, but this time I held on to those few words like a drowning man on to a straw. The bell went, and I moved out to meet Ortiz half-way.

"I remember a dull sound, something almost like

'Dong', and then I was back in a sea of pain. Ortiz's right hand had caught me flush on the ear again. I kept my feet somehow and just punched away at his body. Every time that chopping right came over towards me, I stepped forward to allow it to curl round my neck – doing my ear no good at all, I'm telling you – or I tried to duck under it. Many landed, but every time I felt the shock I thought of my family and my supporters and I just bored in again.

"When the bell ended the ninth round I was numb with pain but my head cleared, and for the first time I knew that I was going to win.

"I thought: 'Mr. Ortiz, if you couldn't knock me out now you'll never do it.' What's more, I could feel Ortiz weakening ever so slightly near the end of that round.

"From the tenth onwards I grew stronger and stronger and Ortiz faded. I never let up in my attacks until the last round. Then I boxed very cautiously. I didn't want a desperate last-minute punch to turn certain victory into defeat."

The last minute of the fight was something never to be forgotten. Spectators were already closing in on the ring in anticipation of a South African triumph and their hoarse exhortations were almost frightening. When the bell ended the fight, bedlam broke loose.

Photographers leapt into the ring. Pappa Toweel somehow propelled his portly body through the ropes and in his headlong dash for his battered but obviously victorious son, fell flat on his face. Flailing his arms wildly, he half-crawled, half stumbled through the throng until he grabbed Vic, who was looking at a loss for the first time that night. Then came the official announcement that Vic Toweel had won the world title, and the pandemonium increased a hundredfold.

Led to his corner and protected from supporters by his seconds and a squad of policemen, Vic said his first words as a world champion. They were:

"My ear is sore!"

When some semblance of order had been restored he

addressed his howling supporters and said: "My only regret is that my mother is not alive to see this."

Manuel Ortiz took his defeat like the true champion he was. "You will stay champion for a long time, Viccie," he said. "You are the fastest thing on two legs I've ever seen. Take care of yourself and take my tip: Rest a lot and don't fight often."

Then the triumphant Toweels returned to that modest home in Balfour Avenue, Benoni, followed, so it seemed, by three-quarters of the population of Johannesburg.

The new champion was a badly batered young man, and all he wanted was sleep. But that was the only thing his supporters were not willing to grant him. Finally he was taken to a nursing home, where his wounds were dressed. He was given a bed and was soon asleep.

The little Lebanese-South-African said later that it was a dreamless sleep.

Perhaps there were no more dreams for him to dream.

Vic Toweel's victory over Manuel Ortiz must rate amongst the greatest achievements in South African sports history, and it was recognized as such. A night debate was in progress in Parliament in Cape Town but when the news came through of Toweel's win, the late Dr. T.E. Dönges, then Minister for the Interior, interrupted the proceedings and formally announced that a South African had won a world boxing title for the first time. When Vic visited Cape Town not long afterwards he was entertained to lunch in the Parliamentary dining room.

Strangely the fight with its packed stadium made a loss – of £1400, because it took so much to pay Manuel Ortiz to defend his title and because more than £4000 was given away in complimentary tickets.

In his first title defence Vic Toweel thrashed Londoner Danny O'Sullivan, on a TKO in the tenth round after knocking him down fourteen times, a record for a world title fight.

Toweel fought many little fights, including three – one drawn – against Georges Mousse of France and he successfully beat two challengers for his title including the powerful Spaniard, Luis Romero, but there was a fight which he was losing – with his weight. The efforts to keep within the bantamweight limit sapped Toweel's strength. And on top of that he was seeing double regularly. The World Champion was not in good shape.

His defeats by Jimmy Carruthers of Australia shocked South Africa and ended Viccie Toweel's boxing career. His reign as World Champion ended on 15th November, 1952.

Since then there have been other South African World Champions and "World Champions" – brave bantamweight Arnie Taylor who ended his career broke, Peter ("Terror") Mathebula who won the WBA flyweight championship, had several parties and lost his first defence, Gerrie ("I said to myself, 'Ow ow, here comes trouble'") Coetzee who won the WBA heavyweight title, Piet Crous, and now Brian Mitchell, the action man who can whip the best and who would certainly be right up there with the great champions if he were given a fair chance to campaign universally.

One of the astonishing things about boxers is that so many of them seem genuine sportsmen. Manuel Ortiz was. The man who had gone to Mass with Viccie Toweel before the fight also visited his vanquisher in hospital after the fight – and gave him a suit. "You're a champ now and you have to look the part."

There was great excitement in 1984 when the Wallabies won all four of their tests of their tour of the British Isles and Ireland. The All Blacks have performed the feat once. The Springboks did it on four successive tours and would, without a shadow of doubt, have added to that number if they had been allowed the same opportunities to tour as other countries.

The 1951-2 Springboks were the fourth team to tour the UK and Ireland. They were in some ways the happiest of the six Springbok teams which have made the tour, and the most honoured, a cheerful band of rugby players who enjoyed a mild, by British standards, winter and shattered the image of the dour South African which had been built by Bennie Osler's team which plodded through the mud of the 1931-2 season, successful but unloved.

The 1951-2 team had Frank Mellish as manager and Danie Craven as asistant manager. In reality Craven was the coach, the first to go by the name of assistant manager. He coached despite the express intruction of Sport Pienaar, the president of the South African Rugby Board, that he should not coach. But the captain, Basil Kenyon, wanted him to.

The first test would be played at Murrayfield in Edinburgh, the Scottish test ground since 1925.

The run-up to the test had not been uniformly smooth. There had been the two-point win over Cardiff with a Chum Ochse try in five minutes from time, the unedifying battle of Stradey Park when the Springboks met Llanelli, the loss of Basil Kenyon with an eye injury at Pontypool Park, and then defeat by London Counties at Twickenham when the Springboks chaired their opponents from the field.

After the London Counties match there would be a match at Oxford and a match at Aberavon, in Wales and then the first test up in the Scottish capital. And Scotland were the only one of the Home Unions which had defeated the Springboks and that back in 1906 when they beat Paul Roos's team, captained that day by Paddy Carolin, 6-0 in the first international the Springboks had ever played abroad.

In fact nothing suggested the drama that was to follow as the Springboks moved up from Port Talbot in Wales. Their captain, Basil Kenyon, lay in St. George's Hospital in London where an operation saved the sight of his right eye, and Hennie Muller was now the captain with Fonnie du Toit, the scrum half who played 22 of the 31 matches on the tour, the new vice-captain. These two with Frank Mellish and Danie Craven would pick the Springbok team for the test against Scotland.

Scotland did not expect disaster either. The *Voice of Scotland* had called the Springboks' play childish when they defeated Glasgow and Edinburgh in their only visit north of the Tweed prior to the test. This evoked a cable from South Africa to Craven, "Come home. Bring children with you. All forgiven." *The Voice* sang a different tune after the Murrayfield affair.

Dick Stent goes on to describe the proceedings in his book *The Fourth Springboks:*

> Whoever chose North Berwick, some twenty-odd miles from Edinburgh on the Firth of Forth, as the place for the Springboks to spend the week before their first international against Scotland did them a great service.
>
> Their hotel had as happy an atmosphere as any met on the tour and there was every facility on the spot for carrying out Craven's prescription for physical and mental fitness.
>
> He suggested as much golf as possible – there are three lovely courses at North Berwick – with one brisk walk in the morning and one in the evening. So lovely was the countryside that none ever felt these walks to be chores – in fact, everyone looked forward to them – particularly the picturesque route over rolling meadows along the seaside to the ruins of Tantallon Castle, which dates back to the fourteenth century.

The team to play at Murrayfield was chosen early in the week – on the Tuesday evening after the players had had a light run on a school ground near by. The big surprise was the omission of "Chum" Ochse, who many felt would be the first choice as a wing. Particularly did such a view gain ground when his fine tries against Cardiff and Llanelly earlier in the tour were remembered.

It was said that he was passed over because of a weakness in defence, but this was revealed only in the first match in which he played – against South-Western Counties at Plymouth – and this was at a time when several of those chosen had not come on the form which they had subsequently developed. Geffin's selection was assured by some fine place-kicking at practice, and the selectors' attention must have been drawn to it by the shrill cheers of the schoolboys watching him with attention and keen appreciation!

When the side was announced sixteen names were given, the additional one being Dennis Fry, who was an alternative to Lategan at centre. It was to be Fry's fate to have this happen to him in four of the five internationals of the tour, and on each occasion he was not to play.

On this occasion, manager Mellish did not give the selectors' final decision until the two players were sitting side by side at lunch in Edinburgh before the game. His task was thus made the easier as he was able to break it to both at once. I happened to be on the spot at the time from the way Lategan's ears reddened I concluded the bad news must have been for him! But he said afterwards that it was "because Dennis had not been chosen", and both these two model sportsmen took the situation in a splendid way.

The fifteen that eventually played then differed in only two respects from the side which had beaten Aberavon and Neath. It was decided that Buchler was fit enough to stand the strain of the match and he replaced Keevy at full-back, and Johnstone came in for Ochse on the left wing.

Delport had been consistently the better hooker – although always insisting that "Piet (Wessels) is my superior" – du Rand had to be in the pack somewhere, and lock seemed his best place. Koch was probably the first choice for the forwards, and van Wyk and Stephen Fry were the best of the flankers on form.

The morning of the match Craven, Hennie Muller, and Fonnie du Toit went to have a look at Murrayfield. The weather was fine, the field firm if heavy.

Hennie Muller said to Craven, "Doc, we're going to thump them by double figures."

Craven did not like that. "You can't say that sort of thing before a test."

But Hennie Muller was determined, "This ground is just like Newlands. We'll eat them here."

In the interim between the announcement of the team and the match Delport developed a boil on his neck, but this quickly cleared up, and Stephen Fry tested a strained thigh muscle to find it sound again.

As the day drew nearer there seemed to be a growing confidence in the Springbok camp, and several little episodes emphasised this. One was the small celebration in the "Orange Room", (the team's common-room, so-called because there was always a sack of oranges there for the players to pick from) on the birth of a daughter to the wife of Willem Barnard in Pretoria.

Another was the jocularity which greeted the letters, to every player, containing a card from Major B. Baines, of Cape Town. Stuck to each was a hair of the sanda-wane, a Central African wolf, which had the reputation of bringing good luck to all who received it. It was claimed that it had helped the Springbok cricket team win the first Test match in England earlier in the year.

Scotland's hopes were buoyed up by the recollection of their victory the previous year at Murrayfield of 19 points to nil over Wales. Nine of that inspired team were in the Scottish side again – Scott, Rose and Cameron among the backs, and Taylor, Kininmonth, Elliot, Dawson, Inglis and Wilson among the forwards.

Taylor, Kininmonth and Elliot were the back row against Wales and it was said that they performed wonders. But Scotland, who had already been beaten by France, subsequently went down to Ireland and England and ended up by sharing the lowest position in the 1950-1 championship table. In this match it appeared that Scotland did not expect to win the set scrums (indeed, one critic said that it was a waste of a player to have a specialist hooker!), for, although selected with an eye on the scale, the home pack averaged ten pounds per man less than the 120-stone Springbok eight. Their main hopes were to do well in the loose and for their fly-half, Angus Cameron – a match-winning player on his day – to strike form.

Scotland got the biggest thrashing in the history of international rugby. One of the discussion points that followed the Springboks' 44-nil victory was whether or not this could be regarded as a record. The general verdict was that it was a record of recognised internationals.

In 1906, it was recalled, Paul Roos's Springboks ran up a 55-6 score against France. But that match was hardly more than an exhibition; it was before France had seriously entered the international circle, and the spectacle was remembered of Frenchmen standing still and applauding the Springbok movements and their rhythmic execution.

On this occasion there was no score for the first seventeen minutes of the game, but in the next hour of play the wildly-inspired Springboks scored seven goals, two tries and one dropped goal, without even the suggestion of a reply from the disconcerted Scots.

It was a complete rout – a rout organised by the exercise of first, method, and then genius.

Murrayfield's great crowd of over 70, 000, who had started the day by exhorting their team with the traditional cry of "Feet, Scotland, Feet", stood at the end in homage to one of the finest all-round displays of rugby ever witnessed on the international field. Jock Wemyss, the old Scottish international, said, "Never have I seen such a superb pack of forwards. This side has restored the full grandeur of Springbok rugby."

The storming pack, having limbered up with a quick bloodwarming exercise before they took the field, immediately took command of the forward battle. But Brewis plugged the touchline until his backs had found their feet. Then he set them in motion.

Immediately the whole machine was in full roar. We saw backs and forwards tearing down the field in handling movements that would have done credit to professional jugglers. One Scot said afterwards, "It was like an avalanche", and certainly all the life seemed to have been pressed out of the home team in the second half.

For a while there was silence over Murrayfield as the Scots beheld the extent of their defeat. One in front of Craven said, Well, we're getting a thrashing but let's sit back and enjoy rugby, because look how these Springboks are playing. I'm going to count the number of passes in the next scoring movement." He counted 28 when Basie van Wyk, broken nose and all, scored and 32 when Hennie Muller scored under the posts.

As one observer put it, "They seemed like men wandering around in a foreign town", and in the last spell I felt that the Springboks, had they chosen to chase after it, could have brought the tally up to the half-century. The Scots defence had completely crumpled then and only accidental collisions and bumps held their line intact on about four or five occasions in the last quarter of an hour.

It is difficult to single out any member of the Springbok side as chiefly responsible for the scintillating display, though the guiding hand of Brewis was always recognisable. It was a symptom of the equal part that all played that no fewer than eight of the side scored a try. Brewis dropped a goal and Koch, who was, incidentally, the most frequently prominent forward, was the only man to score twice.

Indeed, there was a precision about the passing among the forwards that would have been the envy of any three-quarter, and the backing-up and capacity to counter-attack reached heights not yet seen before on the tour.

The last signs of fight from the Scottish side came from the pack, who did well to win 23 of 5 line-out and 8 of 27 scrums; for Delport, who played his best game of the tour, had the benefit of a great heave every time the ball went along that "imaginary line".

Penalties were few and far between and it is pleasing to record that there were only five in the whole match - four being awarded to Scotland and one to South Africa.

Buchler must have a special mention for his faultless display at full-back. Before the match he told a friend that if he could have a feel of the ball in the first minute he knew he would be all right. It came his way just after the kick-off, he took it surely and found a good touch and he did not do a wrong thing all the afternoon. His kicking was designed to find certain, if not long, touches, his handling was immaculate, his tackling sound and his going down on a rolling ball fearless.

Johnstone was ubiquitous and resourceful, and once he took part in the same movement on three occasions - first he came into the line from his blind-side position, took a reverse pass and careered back to be there for a final transfer when the movement swung the other way.

Lategan's drawing of his man was always timed to a nicety and it was this that helped van Schoor, using an inside swerve not always associated with his game, to make some startling breaks. Marais ran hard and threateningly every time he had the ball.

Brewis showed that he was "a worthy descendant of Bennie Osler", as one critic hailed him, and Fonnie du Toit played with snap and intelligence at scrum-half.

Geffin goaled seven of nine attemps at conversions and Koch cut through the Scottish defence on several occasions like a bulldozer heaving soft terrain – only at a greater pace! Dinkelmann and du Rand were the men behind the line-out success and du Rand also played splendidly in the loose.

Van Wyk performed miracles when it is remembered that he played more than half the game with a broken nose. Stephen Fry must be singled out as the first forward to bring the crowd to its feet, which he did with a great break-through, and Muller's backing-up, fine tackling and tear-away runs marked him once again as an outstanding number eight.

On the Scots side there must be a saving clause for Burrell at full-back, and his tackling was not the irresolute thing that we saw from some of his team-mates. Cameron, at fly-half, never really had a chance to get under way, but in the Scottish pack there was always Douglas Elliot, often, it seemed, fighting a lone battle.

"One could not help sympathising with young Angus Cameron, who was captaining the side from the fly half position, and I found myself telling him several times when I came near him: 'Get your forwards together. Tell them to stop our forwards from coming away in the loose,' said Hennie Muller afterwards.

"Poor Cameron just looked at me. It seemed to me folly to appoint a back as captain, and this Murrayfield slaughter certainly proved it. The Scottish forwards, with the exception of Elliot, were hopelessly outclassed, with no one to provide the clarion call of defiance." The Springbok forwards scored seven of the nine tries scored that afternoon.

It seems strange to recall, in considering the final result, that the first side likely to score was Scotland, when Elliot broke through and Rose was only held up near the line. But Stephen Fry brought his side back with a fifty-yard dash through the centre and Brewis had an early put for goal.

The Springboks did not score in the first quarter of an hour, but it was obvious during that period that they were getting on top. Then, from a line-out, S. Fry obtained and broke away. He passed to Marais, who slipped back a reverse pass to Fry, who gave to du Rand, who forced his way over for a try which Geffin failed to convert (3-0). Within two minutes South Africa scored again. First, Koch broke through from a line-out and a score was only averted by Marais failing to get to a hard pass.

From the subsequent scrum Brewis sold Cameron a perfect dummy, snapped a pass to Lategan, who fed van Schoor after he had drawn the defence perfectly. Van Schoor, noticing the defence tearing over towards Johnstone on his wing, cut in and caught them on the wrong foot. He scored close in and Geffin converted to make the score 8-nil.

The tally became 13-nil after twenty-four minutes, when Koch booted the ball across the line and touched down for Geffin to convert, and though van Wyk left the field shortly afterwards with a broken nose, the Springboks kept up the pressure.

Brewis dropped a goal and it was 16-nil, and then van Wyk returned to lead a forward rush which took the ball into the Scottish "25". Here, from a scrum, Brewis cut in, passed to du Rand, who gave to Koch, who almost roamed over for an easy try. The half-time score was 19-nil.

Shortly after the start of the second half a loose maul formed, Delport obtained and broke past two men as if they were not there, to score an unexpectedly simple try, which Geffin converted to make the score 24-nil. Then Geffin came through, passed to Stephen Fry, who gave to van Wyk, who shook off two would-be tacklers, to score a try which Geffin converted.

Then du Rand broke through and kicked high ahead. Van Wyk was there to boot it on and Muller came from "nowhere" to score between the posts. Geffin converted and it was 34-nil after seventeen minutes' play in the second half. Two minutes later the Springboks scored again. Scott dropped a pass and Lategan flashed up, gathered and, in an individual run of fifty yards, beat Burrell and scored under the posts, Geffin converting again to make it 39-nil.

South Africa kept up the pressure and Johnstone, Lategan and Dinkelmann brought play on to the Scottish line with a passing bout, after which Dinkelmann obtained and barged his way over at the corner. Geffin converted with a great kick and it was 44-nil.

Some afterthoughts were:

Thirteen was lucky: It was the thirteenth match of the tour, it was thirteen years since South Africa had last played a Test match, it was the thirteenth international they had played in the British Isles (there was, of course, no one in the side with the jersey number 13).

The Juggernaut has wings: This was the verdict of the *Cape Times,* who remembered the favourite term of many English writers for the Springboks.

"Good for Scotland": This was what the bus conductor told me on the way home from Murrayfield. "It will take some of the starch out of the old school ties," he said – this last remark, made with a wink, being a reference to the fact that so many of the Scottish rugby clubs are "former pupils".

"Flodden was not in it" was the opinion of his colleague, who said: "It was Bannockburrn in reverse!"

Edinburgh Castle's tribute: The Castle was floodlit on the Saturday night of the match. I was told that this was to honour the Springbok visit, but, as it happened, it seemed to make the victory shine even more brightly!

Here is some comment on the game which shows that the overseas pressmen pulled no punches:

Frank Shaw, London *"Sunday Express":* Never in modern times has an international fifteen been so utterly outplayed, so routed and humiliated as Scotland were before their own Murrayfield crowd by the dazzling Springboks. Nine tries tell their own story of a game so one-sided that Scotland's frantic attemps to stop the rout bordered on pathos."

D.R. Gent, *Sunday Times:* "South Africa played most spectacular football, and the combination of the forwards with the backs, and even more of the forwards among themselves, was devastating and delightful."

O.L. Owen *The Times:* "The going was soft and slippery, but from start to finish much of the South African handling – on as well as off the ground – was first-class, and their running and backing-up had a quality which made the Scottish effort look hopelessly slow and inexpert by comparison."

Charles Bray *Daily Herald:* Those green jerseys were everywhere. The forwards swept down the field with monotonous regularity, sometime dribbling, sometimes passing the ball among each other with lightning rapidity."

H.L.V. Day *Sunday Chronicle:* "It was team work of a superlative order which routed Scotland, the short passing being as fine as anything I have seen."

Terence O'Connor *Sporting Chronicle:* "This South African pack has changed the accepted version of forward play. They are not just the means of getting the ball to their backs for them to do the scoring, as is the case in British rugby. Every player is an attacker."

E.W. Swanton *Daily Telegraph:* "Almost from the moment of the first try there appeared between the two sides such a wide and ever-growing disparity that the game developed merely into an exhibition . . . the South African backs had a much greater share in the success than might be supposed from the bare narrative. The understanding between Du Toit and Brewis generally ensured that no clear chance should go to waste, and it was the speed over the first few yards of Brewis that so frequently made his centres a danger."

The truth is the Scottish team was hopelessly unprepared. We were astonished afterwards to learn that the first Scottish trial of the season was held nearly three weeks later (on December 15) and the final trial on December 24!

That match in 1951 had a devastating effect on Scottish

rugby. They went on to lose the next fourteen internationals in a row, winning again only in February, 1955.

The score, 44-0, was a record for official internationals, surpassing the 38-0 defeat the Springboks inflicted on Ireland in 1912. In the eyes of many it is still a record, though there are those who believe that Ireland's 60-0 defeat of Romania in 1986 surpasses it and since then, of course, there have been the funny scores at the "World" Cup which make a nonsense of the record books.

Just to refresh memories the Springbok touring team in 1951-2 was:

Fullbacks: Johnny Buchler (Transvaal) and Jakkals Keevy (Eastern Transvaal).

Wings: Chum Ochse (Western Province), Buks Marais (Boland), Cowboy Saunders (Border), Paul Johnstone (Western Province).

Centres: Tjol Lategan (Western Province), Ryk van Schoor (Rhodesia), Des Sinclair (Transvaal), Basie Viviers (OFS).

Fly halves: Hansie Brewis (Northern Transvaal), Dennis Fry (Western Province).

Scrum halves: Fonnie du Toit (Northern Transvaal), Hansie Oelofse (Transvaal).

Props: Chris Koch (Boland), Okey Geffin (Transvaal), Jaap Bekker (Northern Transvaal), Frans van der Ryst (Transvaal).

Hookers: Willie Delport (Eastern Province), Piet Wessels (OFS).

Locks: Jan Pickard (Western Province), Ernst Dinkelmann (Northern Transvaal), Gert Dannhauser (Transvaal), Willem Barnard (Griqualand West).

Flanks: Stephen Fry (Western Province), Basie van Wyk (Transvaal), Ben Myburgh (Eastern Transvaal), Salty du Rand (Rhodesia).

Number 8's: Basil Kenyon (Border – captain), Hennie Muller (Western Province – vice-captain).

Manager: Frank Mellish.

Assistant Manager: Danie Craven.

The National Selectors in 1951: Bill Schreiner (chairman), Bill Zeller, Frank Mellish, Bert Kipling, and Geoff Gray.

CHEETHAM'S BABES

When the South African team was chosen for the Australasian tour of 1952-3, they were suggestions that the tour be cancelled because it was such a weak side. South African cricket had never been a mighty force when compared to Australia and England, and now it looked weaker than ever. Jack Cheetham's team was destined to do the Charles Atlas trick, and sand would stop being kicked in the face of South African cricket. What happened on that tour was dramatic, heroic, and a watershed.

South Africa's record against England was mediocre before the Second World War with only one won test in England in 1935. After the War things were no better – thrashed by England home and away in 1947 and 1949, and then crushed by Australia in 1949. In 1951 South Africa had her second test win in England but they lost the series 3-1. South African cricket was not healthy.

Then when the team was chosen to go to Australia at the end of the next year there were players no longer available who were household names even in the rickety world of South African cricket: Dudley Nourse, Bruce Mitchell, Alan Mellville, the Rowan brothers, Cuan McCarthy, Clive van Ryneveld, Tufty Mann, Geoff Chubb, and George Fullerton. And they were to take on the might of Australia who had not lost a series since Jardine and bodyline in the early thirties, Australia with mighty names like Ray Lindwall, Keith Miller, Arthur Morris, Neil Harvey, Syd Barnes, Lindsay Hassett, Ken Archer, Bill Johnston, Ian Johnson, Richie Benaud, Sam Loxton, Ian Craig, Colin McDonald, Don Tallon and Doug Ring.

South Africa had only once beaten Australia in 26 tests since 1902, and managed a draw in only three others. The 1949-50 Australians, captained by Lindsay Hassett, who had succeeded the might Don Bradman after his triumphant tour of England, won four of the five tests with a drab draw in the fourth test, and that was in South Africa.

No wonder people suggested that the Springboks should stay at home in 1952. After all who would watch such a rag-tag lot of youngsters which Jack Cheetham captained and Ken Viljoen managed? The South African Cricket Union had to guarantee £10 000 against a financial loss by their hosts of the Australian Cricket Board.

The Springboks were too dull to attract crowds in their opening matches, and a financial loss seemed assured. Worse, the Aussies felt sorry for them and famous players from the past, including Sir Don, tried to help. But there was one man who had faith – Jack Cheetham, who had always wanted to captain South Africa at cricket, and now had his chance. From the start he believed that his young Springbok side could do what nobody else had done – beat the Australians and do it on their own paddocks.

One way to succeed is to try harder than the opposition. The Springboks did that. They got fit and they fielded, not perfectly, but well enough to change the cricketer's concept of fielding and in the process to draw people to the grounds, just to watch them field.

They got to the first test with no real victories and defeat at the hands of New South Wales by five wickets. Yet they surprised lots of people by losing the first test at the Woolloongabba ground in Brisbane by only 96 runs. The difference between the two teams was effectively Neil Harvey. He scored 109 and 52.

The team went south from the oppressive heat for the second test in Melbourne, the team's favourite city. Cheetham won the toss and after being 9/2 in their first innings the Springboks won the test by 82 runs after Russell Endean had scored 162 not out and Tayfield had taken 13/165 in the match.

During the match Endean took what Louis Duffus describes as 'the most amazing catch I have ever seen'. Miller hoisted Tayfield down to long on, and it was going for an easy six when Endean on the boundary leapt into the air with one arm extended to its fullest. He caught the ball, and Miller said something best described as 'By Jove, he's caught it!' And this time there were people there to see it. 120 000 were at Melbourne Cricket Ground to watch the test. The tour was assured of success. It was South Africa's second test win over Australia ever.

The third test was at Sydney Cricket Ground, home to Miller and Lindwall. They bowled the Springboks out twice, and Harvey scored 190 for Australia to win by an innings and 38 runs. South African cricket had slumped back to its predictable mediocrity it seemed.

It was hot and humid at Adelaide Oval for the fourth test. Lindsay Hassett made 162, McDonald 154, Neil Harvey 84 and 116 but Miller and Lindwall broke down, did not get a wicket and took no further part in the series. The match was drawn. One down and one to play. No post-war team had done as well against the Australians, anyway.

Viccie Toweel lost to Jimmy Carruthers but the Springboks found batting form against Victoria, Anton Murray was back from an appendectomy but Jackie McGlew was out with a finger fracture.

The Springbok selection committee had difficulty selecting the team, especially as McGlew and Endean had opposed ideas about the last two places. Jack Cheetham did not announce his team till the morning of the fifth test in Melbourne. Roy McLean got the nod though there was speculation that he might have been dropped, and his selection was largely due to the excellence of his fielding.

The Aussies had problems – Miller and Lindwall were out of the team. The Springboks believed that they could win.

There is nobody better qualified to take us through the test match than Jack Cheetham himself. The following account is from Cheetham's book, *Caught by the Springboks:*

At our team talk, before walking down to the ground, I stressed the fact that we were in better fettle than the Australians, to win the Test. For the first time in the Series, our batsmen could play shots, confident in the ability of those following to get runs. Our slip catching had, in the past three games, been outstanding, and our

110

fielding was being maintained at its high level. I was quite sure that we could, and would, win the match, and it was up to us all to give just that little bit extra, so that we could become the first team to hold the Australians since Jardine's side of the 'Bodyline Era' in 1932-33.

As we walked quietly down to the ground, each and everyone of us experienced that feeling of expectation – this was what we had battled for through some heart-breaking days on the tour. Our arrival at the ground coincided with that of the umpires – Mel McInnes and Ron Wright having been retained for the game.

The pitch surrounds were very wet, and Lindsay Hassett and I decided to play, after the curator and his staff had again miraculously mopped up the numerous small pools. It was eighty minutes after the scheduled time, which left only twenty-five minutes of play before lunch. The toss was again important – this Test was to be played over six days, and with a Sunday in between, meant that whoever lost the toss could anticipate a final innings on a seven day old wicket.

The spinning coin descended on to the black coloured wicket, and seemed to stand on the edge – slowly turning over. It lay there, almost mockingly, and as Lindsay picked it up, I wondered what he would do. He had no hesitation about batting though, and as we walked through the gate, I remarked how much we had enjoyed the Series, and hoped that our last Test would be the best and happiest game of all.

I hoped, naturally, that the wicket might be lively after the rain, but for once the Melbourne wicket failed to live up its reputation. The heavy atmosphere helped the bowlers to move the ball, but the pitch was slow and easy. There was no early sensation, although Morris twice edged deliveries from Fuller on to his pads, and McDonald played an iffish shot down to third man off Watkins' bowling.

It was ten minutes before tea when the first wicket fell – McDonald lifting a ball from Mansell deep, for McLean fielding at long-on, to take a good catch. The score was 122, McDonald's share being 41, and it was the highest opening partnership of the Series.

Harvey followed, and used his feet well to move freely up the wicket to the spinners. It seemed as if he was starting from where he had left off at Adelaide, but when three, he played over a ball from Tayfield which kept low, and hit Waite midway up the pads, with Harvey out of his ground. It was rotten luck for both bowler and wicketkeeper, and a quick wicket then would have been to our advantage.

The rarity of left-handed batsmen in South African cricket, seems to have reaped a harvest in the inability, to a large extent, of our bowlers to pin such batsmen down – at all events Morris and Harvey played freely, scoring quickly, and forcing our bowlers into errors of direction and length by the manner in which they cut, drove and turned the ball. Quick bowling changes had no effect, and in twenty minutes after tea, 30 runs had been added to the score, before Morris lost his wicket through an act of sportsmanship, which one rarely sees in Test cricket.

From a shortish delivery off Murray's bowling, Harvey pushed a ball into the covers and ran. Morris sent him back, or tried to, but Harvey continued running, eventually ending up five yards from Morris when Watkins fielded the ball. Arthur immediately ran past Harvey and the batsman had barely crossed over when Waite broke the wicket. His score stood at 99, and he had not enjoyed a good season from the run-getting point of view, many sportswriters suggesting that he should be omitted from the team to go to England. What a temptation it must have been for Arthur to stand, as he was justified in doing – we were all sorry to see his splendid innings terminated in such an unfortunate manner.

Undeterred, Harvey continued to take toll of the bowling, and partnered by his captain, raced towards his fifty. Hassett settled down quickly, and he too, with glances and cuts helped the score along. The 200 went up, and shortly afterwards the new ball became due, although its use merely served to increase the rate of scoring.

Tayfield, Murray, Mansell and Keith were all tried, the latter just before close, but they made no impression on the batsmen, and when stumps were drawn, their two wickets had fallen for 243 runs – a good beginning for Australia, which put them in a strong position.

I believe that there were many people who gave us little hope after the first day's play – although we weren't upset about their total. The attitude in the team was that the wicket would not be of any greater assistance to their bowlers, and that our batsmen too would score many runs.

Saturday morning turned out fine and cool, and when we arrived at the ground, there were queues of spectators waiting for the gates to open. It was a cheering sight, and when, as we were busy practising, thousands upon thousands poured into the stands, we knew that any doubts we might have had regarding the success of the tour financially, could be dispelled.

The brilliant batting of Harvey, and the inclusion of Craig in the Australian side, drew a crowd of over 47 000 people – a record attendance for any South African match, and it was a thrill in itself just looking at the multitude of people grouped around the field.

In the morning session, we had early success, when, after a cautious opening period, Hassett played a ball off Watkins' bowling into the gully. Endean at second slip raced for it, and Harvey called for a run – Hassett momentarily hesitated, and then tore up the wicket, but Endean's direct hit on the stumps found Hassett out of his ground – 268 for 3, and the last man had scored 40 runs.

Harvey, in the meantime, was pushing the score along, and treated the spinners severely – twice in an over he played that flashing square cut off Mansell's bowling, one being stopped inches from the fence, and the other sped through to the boundary. Then he

113

played a shot that I like to think of as the greatest I have ever seen by than gifted batsmen. Mansell held the ball back, flighting it a little more than normally – Harvey walked down the wicket and started a drive, only to find the ball dropping short of his bat. Merely turning the bat over in his wrists, without in the least checking the shot, he glanced the ball down to fine leg for three runs. I venture to say that nine hundred and ninety-nine batsmen out of a thousand would have either lifted the ball back to the bowler or checked the drive, ending the stroke with a desperate prod at the ball, whereas Neil's reactions were so quick, and his wrist play so controlled, that he was not in the least upset when the ball dropped short.

There were times when our fielding was loose – not generally, but in isolated cases, and with only three wickets down, and a huge total on the board, it was not altogether surprising. When Harvey gets on top of the bowling, it is a difficult job trying to check the flow of shots, and fielding was a gruelling business, as the batsmen gave us no let up.

Craig, playing very correctly, was the first to go. The cheering crowd, who acclaimed his maiden half-century, had scarcely settled back, with visions of the other half being completed, when, with the score at 417, he lifted a cover-drive off Fuller's bowling, which went straight into Keith's hands at cover point – Headley made no mistake with the catch.

Craig had played a splendid innings, and, although overshadowed by Harvey at times, showed indeed that he has great batting gifts. Harvey was thrashing the ball to all parts of the field, and was uncanny in the placing of his shots. With the scoreboard reading 199 opposite his name, the addition of a single brought the crowd to its feet, and he received a terrific cheer. It was his first double century in first class cricket, and his eighth century against South Africa in Test Matches.

In attempting to hit a slower ball from Fuller over cover-point's head, Harvey skied it, and it fell midway between McLean and me. We both went for it, and I got there first, standing on his foot when he attempted to take the catch. I told Roy later that if he had caused me to miss it, I would have kicked him round the ground, but he insists that it was the finger he got to the ball, which helped me to hold the catch. The score was 450 for 5, and Harvey's share was 205 runs – he had batted seven and a quarter hours, and reached the boundary 19 times.

In reviewing the Tests, I can't help shuddering at the thought of Harvey coming in to bat – he had scored 827 runs in 8 innings against us – it just wasn't cricket.

Eventually the Australian innings closed for 520 runs.

Tayfield, with 3 wickets for 129 runs, had shouldered the major portion of our attack, and his total of wickets in the Series – 27 – constituted a record for a South African playing against Australia. Hugh certainly deserved the honour, he had carried the bowling throughout the tour, and never failed to impress as being an outstanding performer with the ball.

A feature of the play was the fact that John Waite had not conceded any byes in the innings, a tribute to his fine wicket keeping.

There was an hour left for play, and Waite and Endean opened our batting against the "New" Australian attack – Noblet and Archer. The occasion was a big one for both, as their performances in this match would determine their chances of a trip to England. It was perhaps this thought that caused Noblet to depart from his usual accuracy, and he did not impress, bowling wide of the off stump.

Both batsmen were soon off the mark, and seemed quite comfortable against the attack. There was not the same air of tension even in the dressing room as usual, because of the absence of Lindwall and Miller, and Pop Norton exclaimed "That's a cream puff" when Archer tried to bounce a ball at Waite, who ducked without undue haste, under the very short pitched delivery.

115

A superb drive through the covers for four, and a late-cut, which brought two runs, by Waite, pushed the score along, and then Endean played two beautiful on-side drives to catch up with his partner. Hassett made a change bringing Johnston on, and it proved a successful move, as Endean played at a widish ball, snicking it low down on the off, for Langley to bring off a smart one-handed catch. Of the 31 runs scored, Endean's share was 16, and the fielders crowded round John Watkins as he faced up to the first deliveries from Johnston.

Waite was not perturbed, however, and frequent bowling changes did not cramp his batting at all – he scored freely, and when Ring was brought on to bowl the last over of the day, used his feet well to score from drives through the covers. When stumps were drawn, our total stood at 48 for 1 – and we still had an awfully long way to go.

Ken Viljoen and I were at the hotel that night, when we were reminded of our remarks at Adelaide. Sir Donald Bradman was in Melbourne, attending the Australian Board of Control meeting, which was being held to decide on all aspects of the Australian tour of England. He came over to us in the foyer, and remarked that we were certainly going about our winning of the match the hard way, as Lindwall and Miller weren't there to beat us this time.

At least we weren't downhearted about the big score – we had all done our best, and had no excuses. I do know this though, all the batsmen were confident of their ability to get runs, and the Aussies weren't going to have things all their own way.

It was raining again, as I looked out of the window of my room on Monday morning, and the squally weather continued all day. Another good crowd had gathered, as Johnston and Archer opened the bowling to Waite and Watkins.

Johnny Waite was never in trouble, and played each ball in the middle of the bat. To overcome Johnston's

116

leg-stump attack, he took guard outside the leg stump, and drove the ball into the covers with graceful shots.

Waite, playing easily his best innings of the series, had passed his previous highest score of 62, and drove a ball from Johnston to mid-off wide of Harvey, who, he thought was beaten by the speed of the ball. He called for a run, and was half way down the track, when Harvey picked the ball up one-handed, to throw the wickets down, with Waite a yard out of his crease. Lunch was taken then, with the score at 129 for 2, Waite's contribution being 64.

Perhaps the strain of waiting out the lunch period without having faced a ball, and yet due at the crease immediately after it, forced Funston on the defensive when play re-commenced. In striking contrast to Watkins, who treated each ball on its merits, and soon reached his 50, Funston patted the ball down the wicket, adding to his score by means of singles.

Funston, when 16, was beaten by Johnston's swing and out l.b.w. with the score at 189 – although a laboured innings, he and Watkins had added 60 very valuable runs, and paved the way for a big total.

Headley Keith walked slowly to the wickets, and was plainly nervous in his first Test innings. He quietly played out the over, and after a quiet chat with Watkins in the middle of the pitch, took up his position at the bowling end, to see his partner dismissed in a most unfortunate manner, when eight runs short of a century.

Archer, taking over from Noblet, bowled a ball wide of the off-stump, and Johnny, possibly a bit upset at the previous wicket falling, with his score at 92, played a hasty shot at the ball, mishitting it and dragging it on to his wicket. It was an unfortunate end to a splendid innings, in which he had, after a cautious start, really got on top of the bowling.

With the score standing at 189 for 4, McLean joined Keith – and began an exhibition of aggressive batting seldom seen in cricket. Starting confidently, he was off the mark with a drive on the onside, and square cut

117

Archer vigorously next ball. When Johnston – recognised as our only real danger in the bowling department – dropped a ball short, Roy almost broke the fence palings with a powerful hook, and repeated the stroke twice more to notch additional fours. He just could not be subdued, and played a scintillating cover-drive which Harvey partially stopped, for McDonald to cut off a few yards from the fence.

When Keith was inveigled into hitting across a slower ball from Johnston and bowled, the partnership had added 50 runs – Keith having scored 10, the score stood at 239 for 5, and we still had a long way to go when I joined McLean.

As if to welcome me with an exhibition of how to treat all bowling, he proceeded to lambaste the attack to all parts of the ground. Brought on instead of Archer, Benaud found to his cost that McLean doted on spin bowling. The first ball was square cut past point for 2 runs – the next was lifted wide of mid-on for 4, than a mighty straight drive put the ball into the crowd next to the screen. As we passed in the middle of the pitch, I murmured "Steady son", so he obligingly patted the next ball back to the bowler, and, as if remorseful at his sudden weakness, crashed the next delivery through the crowded covers, the ball passing between the fielders, to quote John Arlott – "like an express train through a suburban station."

The crowd literally screamed, and when Roy took a smart single off the last ball of the over, I was not the only happy one at the thought that he had the strike, as all of us, even the Australian team, were enjoying his masterly display.

In 35 minutes, we added 50 runs to the score – my share being nine, but the advent of Noblet, vice Johnston, saw the partnership broken. One of his deliveries, pitched on the off stump, came back off the wicket, and beat the bat, to just touch the inside edge. Roy had not played forward, and, as the ball keeping low struck his pads, an appeal for l.b.w. was upheld. It was hardly

118

a fair ending to Roy's magnificent innings, which had only occupied 93 minutes, and of the 101 runs added to the total, he had scored 81 – it had seemed as if nothing could dislodge him. As he made his way towards the pavilion, Hassett and Harvey both agreed with me that he had indeed touched the ball, breaking off the conversation to add their plaudits as the crowd rose, giving Roy a tremendous ovation.

I'm afraid that it was a case of "After the Lord Mayor's Show" when Mansell and I settled down to a quiet partnership – the only excitement coming when I tried to drive Ring's slower delivery past him, and lifted the ball slightly. Although the bowler got a hand to the ball, he couldn't complete the catch, and with the total at 325 for 6 wickets, we ended the day's play.

That night, Hugh Tayfield and I spent a pleasant time with Ian and Allie Johnson – it was good to relax in a home again, and if the word cricket was mentioned once, it was by Ian's two sons, who hope to follow in Father's footsteps. Allie really spoilt us that night, and it was with very little time to spare that we reached the hotel – if it hadn't been for the deadline, I think Hugh and I would have stayed there all night.

Hassett took the new ball as soon as possible, entrusting Johnston with the first use of it. Bill really makes the ball move a lot, and his second delivery fizzed across the wicket, hitting Mansell on the thigh. The latter, a stoical person, did not bat an eyelash, but Bill said to me, whilst waiting for the ball to be returned – "You know Jack, I seem to hit an awful lot of people with the new ball." I grinned back and said that he should remember old friends, and not hit me.

Next ball, Mansell turned one past gully for a single, and Bill's first delivery to me, pitched on the off-stump, moving in off the wicket towards the packed leg-side. I lifted by bat and as the ball hit me too, on the thigh – he grinned and called out – "Sorry old man, but I can't help it."

Hassett, in an attempt to break the partnership,

switched Johnston round to the other end – but his slow deliveries were not accurate, and I scored two fours through the leg-trap to reach my 50. Another four to Mansell, off a short ball from Johnston, and the score hurried along – and soon afterwards, he too reached his individual 50, and the scoreboard showed 400.

What was to prove the last over before lunch was bowled by Johnston – a slow delivery trapped Mansell in front, and the seventh wicket fell with the score at 401. Our partnership had realised 111 runs – improving on the record of 91 previously held by Dave Nourse and Sherwell on the Melbourne ground during the 1910-11 tour.

When Tayfield was caught by Ring, the Springboks were 435 all out, giving Australia a lead of 85 runs.

The Australian attack, without Lindwall and Miller, had not greatly impressed the critics. There was certainly not that shock about it, which had made Australia supreme in the past, but Bill Johnston, thrown into the attack time and time again, had looked most likely to take wickets. His in-swingers with the new ball were always dangerous, but he had very little support. In 46 overs he captured 6 wickets for 152 runs, and never gave up trying.

Whilst changing to go on to the field again, I had a quiet talk to the team, stressing the fact that we were within reach of a victory, and that it was up to the fielders to support the bowlers to the hilt, and for the bowlers to maintain accuracy at all times. Indeed, there was an air of eagerness about us as we followed the umpires on the field – throwing the ball about as usual, whilst the batsmen took up their positions.

Fuller's opening over was sensational – his first delivery moved away, for McDonald to play his speciality – the "suicide swish." The ball flew off the bat to Watkins at second slip, and he dropped it! The batsmen took a single, and off the fourth ball of the over, Morris played a cover-drive, lifting the ball, which McLean

Hugh Tayfield catches Richie Benaud off his own bowling after the ball had rebounded off John Watkins at silly mid-on in the 5th test against the Australians in 1953

Above:

Gert Potgieter clears the final hurdle on his way to a world record of 49.7 seconds at the 1958 Empire Games in Cardiff

Right:

Malcolm Spence (left) and Mike Agostini carry Gert Potgieter shoulder high after he had been awarded the trophy for the best performance at the International meeting in Helsinki in 1959. On the left is South African manager Matt Maré

Gary Player with that typical gesture of success as another long putt finds its mark

One of the best stumpings ever seen. Denis Lindsay whips off the bails in the fraction of a second that Colin Cowdrey lifts his foot. This dismissal put the Springboks well on their way to victory in the 2nd test at Trent Bridge in 1965.

attempted to catch, missing the ball altogether which went for two runs. A most difficult chance, but small compensation for the bowler.

With the fielders on their toes, runs had to be wrested from them, and the score rose slowly – at tea-time, after 50 minutes play, there were only 24 on the board. The break seemed to spur us on – especially the bowlers – and after tea, Fuller and Tayfield bowled with a great deal of hostility. The former secured a well-deserved wicket when McDonald, with his score at 11, and the total 36, slashed at a ball outside the off-stump. Watkins more than made up for his earlier lapse, by taking a great one-handed catch, moving two yards over to his right as he did so.

Harvey was soon off the mark, and then Morris was well beaten by Fuller's flighted slower delivery, which he propped back about a foot wide of the bowler. Hampered by a badly bruised heel, Fuller just touched the ball with his finger-tips – whilst throwing himself frantically at the ball. Undeterred, Eddie toiled on, backed by brilliant fielding, as each member of the team excelled himself with magnificent saves.

The turning point of the innings came in Fuller's next over. Bowling to Harvey, he changed his line of attack from the off to the leg stump, and moving the ball off the wicket, bowled Harvey with a ball which the batsman tried to glide. I know how I felt when I saw Neil's back moving towards the pavilion, and can quite appreciate how much of a thrill it was to Eddie. 44 for 2, Harvey out for 7, and the fielders clustering round all talking of a win – "It's in the bag, Skip" they said, and I agreed with them. Indeed, dismissing Harvey – who had scored 834 runs against us in 9 innings – gave our morale such a lift, that anything was possible.

I like to think that no team has ever fielded as we did that day – perhaps it was the fact that the game had swung out way, but we all seemed to have an air of supreme confidence in the outcome, and when play was resumed with Hassett joining Morris – no one fielder outshone the other. It was teamwork at its best – not one man backed up in the field – but three or four; returns to the wicket were bail high, and the bowlers had the upper hand. Neither batsman was happy, although Morris was trying desperately to get on top of the bowling. Twice he ran out to Tayfield, and had to play the ball with his pads, and then, in desperation, he swept a ball perilously near mid-wicket's straining fingers.

Lindsay Hassett was playing a stubborn knock – putting his broad bat in front of each delivery, he never looked worried by the bowling, but he couldn't pierce the field, and scored slowly. Morris raised a cheer when he turned a ball to mid-wicket, where Funston saved a boundary after a thirty yard run.

Then McLean, Murray and Endean, in that order, made great saves through clever anticipation, but slowly the score was raised to 70. Tayfield, tirelessly persistent, forced Morris back on the stumps, for the turn to beat the bat, and the ball to hit him on the pads in front of the wicket. Tayfield and Waite both appealed, the bowler with arms outstretched as he jumped in the air – there was no hesitation on the part of the umpire, and Morris was out for 44 hard earned runs.

The day ended, with Australia, in their second venture, having scored 89 runs for the loss of three wickets, in 155 minutes of batting.

With two days to go, there was still every chance of an outright result being obtained – and, that night, at a small dinner party that Ken and I gave, to repay some of the hospitality that we had been shown in Melbourne, I was very optimistic in my statements.

I called a team meeting the next morning, and impressed on the chaps that we were going to play with one aim, and that was to reach a decision. Irrespective of whether we won or lost, it made no difference, a draw was no use to us at all. I said that our batting had shown up well in the first innings – ten players reaching double figures, and there was no reason why we should be bundled out in our second knock, so that we were, from the start of play that day, going to attack all the time. I ended up – "Listen chaps, it's do or die – and I for one, know it can be done."

Heartened by the news that the bookies were lowering the odds against our winning the match, we took the field grimly determined to force a result.

The first bowling change of the morning was at Fuller's end. He gave way to Mansell, and in an effort to force the batsmen into mistakes, I pushed a silly mid-off and silly mid-on up to Hassett. The seventh ball of Mansell's first over was flighted a little more than usual, and Hassett walked up the wicket, to push forward when the ball dropped a little quicker than he anticipated. Endean – only five yards from the bat – reached down to make the catch look easy – 128 for 4 and Hassett out for 30.

Archer, next in, faced only two balls. The last ball of Mansell's over, he pushed down the wicket, but after Craig had turned a delivery from Tayfield for a single, Archer pushed forward to the next ball, for Watkins, at silly mid-on to fall forward on his elbows to hold a low catch: 129 for 5.

As if scenting the kill, the fielders moved tirelessly, and in stopping a four, McLean ran into the spiked fence uprights, causing a slight tear to the skin on his chest. He hit the fence with such force, that I expected him to be knocked out – and I forced him to leave the field for attention, with Melle taking his place for ten minutes.

The bowlers were not to be denied and Craig skied the ball to mid-wicket, for Endean to hold a great catch, as he ran fifteen yards with his back to the ball. We were sure then that we had a great chance – the score was 152 for 6, and Craig – the last of the re-cognised batsmen was out for 47.

Benaud played out the over safely, and Ring faced up to Mansell's bowling. In the Victorian match, I had acceded to Percy's request that the cover fielders be pushed back for Ring, only to see what would have been a catch to cover off the first ball, land feet short of the deployed fielders. Because of this, when Mansell wanted to move Endean back, I refused to alter the field placing – and Ring obligingly lifted the first delivery to silly mid-on, Endean lunging forward to hold a good catch. 152 for 7 and only Langley, Johnston and Noblet to come – we were truly on top. With that wicket, Hugh had equalled Bedser's record of 30 wickets in the Tests on the 1951 tour, and I was very happy to shake his hand – it was a reward for his never failing accuracy and perseverance.

Benaud then proceeded to exert himself, and played some vigorous drives off Mansell's bowling. Two straight drives for four, caused me to alter the field placing, and at lunch time, he and Langley were still together with the total standing at 168 for 7, a lead of 253 runs.

Eight runs were scored off the first two overs after lunch from Fuller and Watkins, but in Fuller's next over, Benaud cut a ball to Watkins at second slip, and the eighth wicket had fallen for 187 runs. Johnston, obviously a better bat than Noblet, as he once again filled the Number 10 position, stayed long enough to drive an overpitched ball from Watkins to the boundary, before falling to Fuller's slower ball, which he hit hard and straight to me at mid-off. 193 for 9, and the new ball had accounted for two wickets.

The advent of the last man caused Langley to open his shoulders, and in an attempt to cause him to lift the ball, I brought Tayfield on in place of Watkins. Langley played two sparkling cover drives to raise the 200, but when nine runs later Noblet faced up to Fuller's bowling, a faster ball whipped past his bat, to uproot his middle stump. Australia were all out for 209 runs, a lead of 294 runs, with 8 hours of play left.

Eddie Fuller, whose analysis of 30.2 overs, 4 maidens, 66 runs, 5 wickets, had been achieved through his great hearted and tireless bowling, led us off the field to the cheers of the 13 000 spectators, who had appreciated the tense cricket by the manner in which they had accorded their appreciation of the efforts of bowler, batsman or fielder. The Melbourne crowd are a great crowd to play in front of, and they know cricket, in all its aspects.

Johnston and Noblet opened the bowling to Waite and Endean, and the runs came freely. Both batsmen then lapsed into defence, and after some 48 minutes batting, the score at tea was 29 without loss.

Tea seemed to infuse new life into the bowlers, and an anxious period for the batsmen after the interval saw the bowlers well on top. Noblet, indeed, bowled so well that only seven runs came from his first nine overs, and twice he beat Waite – the ball passing outside the off stump. From the anguished reactions of the wicket-keeper and slips, the proverbial coat of paint had separated ball and wicket.

At last the bowler's persistence was rewarded, when, with the score at 42, Waite played a forcing shot off his back foot, for Archer at short mid-on to juggle with the ball, before falling forward to hold the catch. Luck had favoured the fielding side then, but Noblet's accuracy had forced Waite into playing an uppish shot.

Watkins carried on from where his predecessor had left off, and defended dourly – the advent of Ring only seeming to accentuate the ascendancy the bowlers had attained. Few runs were scored, until Endean, sweeping a ball to leg, and Watkins, driving a ball for four runs off the back foot, broke the spell.

Noblet was tiring, and his grip on the batsmen became less pronounced – Watkins late-cutting him beautifully, and Endean scoring with on-drives to mid-wicket. Gradually the score rose, and when Endean reached his half-century, the crowd cheered.

Both batsmen batted soundly towards the close, and, when after first Benaud and then Johnston had failed to effect a separation, stumps were drawn with our score standing at 94, and we required 201 runs to win, with nine wickets in hand.

In retrospect, that evening must have been a pleasant one, but I can remember, as I noted in my diary, that I experienced a tension far greater than ever before. We realised that we had the chance to even the series, an achievement no other touring side had managed since Jardine's 1932-33 team, which had introduced into the game the "body-line" era. It suffices to say that long after leaving Ken Viljoen's room, I lay awake, wondering whether, as in the First Test, we should fall apart, flattering but to deceive, and, then again, hearing a sudden squall of rain, worrying lest nature would deprive us of at least an effort to snatch a win.

There was a very tense atmosphere in the dressing room the next day, and we were all on the field practising busily, half an hour before any of the Australian team made an appearance. As the time approached for the last day's play to start, the air was electric, and players and spectators alike were on edge, when the two leg-spinners opened the Australian attack.

Watkins showed a liking for Ring's bowling, driving a delivery through the covers for four, and then jumping down the wicket to loft the ball just over Johnston's reaching hands at mid-on. Runs came freely, at the rate of a run a minute for the first half hour, and then Hassett made a double change, bringing on Johnston and Archer with the new ball.

Johnston's first over saw the partnership broken – Endean, after playing the first few balls confidently, was well and truly yorked by a ball which seemed to dip in late. He had scored 70 runs out of the total of 124, and had played a dominant innings, in keeping with his great displays throughout the tour. His knock in this innings had tided us over the worst portion, and he had, in his usual unobstrusive way, gathered the runs wherever possible, to shape our innings towards the goal we strived to reach.

Funston, surrounded by fielders, was not a whit put out, and calmly defended his wicket, taking a single off the occasional loose ball. Watkins, ever watchful of the deliveries from Johnston, cut two short balls from Archer to third man, and after only three overs, Hassett brought Noblet on, to join in attack with Johnston. Gradually the batsmen opened out, and with the shine off the new ball, Johnston changed to slow deliveries.

Funston seemed to welcome the change – two cover drives were boundaries all the way, and then with the advent of Ring, Watkins played a beautiful drive through the covers, to reach his half-century. Sitting in the Pavilion, I remarked that I would be happy if Watkins took a single off the next ball bowled – I just didn't like the thought of the half-century on the board, but hardly were the words out of my mouth, before Watkins pushed forward to Ring's next delivery, the ball rebounding from his pad to hit the top of the off-stump. 174 for 3, and still 121 runs required.

John Watkins had played two excellent knocks, and his batting double had been of inestimable value to the team. With scores of 92 and 50, and some magnificent catches, he had indeed played a large part in the team's success. When I, on occasions, chided him for seeming lapses of concentration in the State games, he used to remark that he kept everything for the big stakes – "A thoroughbred, that's me" said John, and I had no leg to stand on after the Fifth Test.

With less than a quarter of an hour to lunch, Keith joined Funston, and opened his account with a beautiful square-cut for four off Ring's delivery. It is a shot that he plays particularly well, and the manner in which he went for the ball, showed that he was grimly determined to get some runs. Both batsmen survived a pre-lunch onslaught from Bill Johnston, who had bowled unchanged for 75 minutes, and they came off the field at lunch-time, not at all grateful for the imposed break in their concentration.

With 115 runs to go, and seven wickets in hand, it is understandable that there was an air of tension in the dressing room. Ken Funston was nervously pacing the room, and Headley Keith sat chair smoking on a bench, not even removing his cap throughout the three quarters of an hour break. Our room attendant had fetched us a light lunch, and as I sat with them, there was a stillness in the room, quite out of keeping with a normal lunch interval.

Although very worked up myself, I tried to ease things for them both, and quietly talked about the coming period of play, telling each how much confidence I had in them to play their part in getting the runs. They were still glum and in a highly strung state, so I turned on the wireless and improvised a Cape "tikkiedraai", which soon had them laughing, and the ice was broken.

The rest of the players returned from their meal, and when play was resumed, we crowded round the windows of the dressing room, watching every ball bowled. Johnston was still plugging away, and with Benaud as his opposite number, the runs came slowly – both batsmen grimly determined in defence, and waiting for an opportunity to gather runs from anything loose.

In the pavilion, Fuller was sitting at the end of the bench counting the score, but, although the scoreboard was in full view, he kept us informed that we needed 108 runs, 107 runs, 105 runs, 104 runs – and with that number still to go, Benaud bowled a top spinner which Funston played no stroke at, for the ball to hit the off-stump. Funston stared down at the wicket, and couldn't believe his eyes – thinking that the ball had rebounded from the 'keeper's pads. There was no doubt though, and there was an uneasy hush in the dressing room as McLean picked up his gloves and bat, and started for the door.

All my gear was next to McLean's, and I moved over to him to wish him luck, murmuring that it was up to him to play his own game, and not throw his wicket away. Roy tugged his cap on and said "Don't worry, Pop, I'll get them for you" – and he certainly did – in a manner which I for one, and all who saw the day's play, will never forget.

Ken Funston, terribly upset, was standing next to me after his good knock, when Benaud bowled the first ball to McLean. Roy swung the ball to mid-wicket, hitting it fairly and squarely in the middle of the bat, and lifting it to Morris twenty-five yards distant. Morris got both hands to the ball, which exploded through them, to bounce on his shoulder and trickle down his back, dropping to the ground. I shall never forget my reaction to the shot – next man in, I stood up, with an empty feeling in the pit of my stomach, only the crowd's groan and excited shout from Anton Murray, allowing me to sink gratefully back on the bench.

Benaud's next delivery was wide, and McLean made a terrific swing at it, missing the ball which ricochetted off his pads just past the stumps. I felt ten years older, and Johnny Waite started to describe the incident, giving a passable imitation of Charles Fortune, as I imagined his commentary to sound at the moment, but when he carried on a ball by ball description, he was howled down from all sides – the dressing room was a silent place, and we all sat, gripped by the thought of what could or could not happen.

Keith took a single off Johnston's next over, and when McLean turned a ball to fine leg to get off the mark, we all relaxed. He pushed back the next few deliveries and then played a straight drive which lofted the ball over the bowler's head, for it to strike the pickets on the second bounce. With Keith, obviously unsettled when Morris, now too close at leg slip missed a sharp chance off Johnston's bowling, playing quietly, McLean picked on Benaud's bowling to cause rounds of applause from the crowd, and I suspect, added a few grey hairs to Hassett's head.

The first ball went for four to long-on, and Hassett waved McDonald round to a position twenty yards from where the ball had dropped. Benaud bowled the next one slightly shorter, so McLean hooked it where McDonald had been fielding, and then pushed the next delivery back to the bowler. The fourth ball was widish, and a sizzling square cut sent it flashing to the boundary – it was a masterly display of intelligent attack, coupled with a freedom of footwork, which few batsmen equal.

With flashing drives, cuts and hooks, McLean kept the scorers working overtime, and Keith too, gathered runs from well controlled drives on the on-side, and vigorous square cuts which sent the ball streaking past the fielders. Gradually the gap dwindled until Fuller's monotonous chant reached 50.

Ring came on for Benaud, and Archer for Johnston, but it was of no avail, and tumultuous applause greeted McLean's 50. There was no stopping the barrage of shots, and when Ring misfielded a drive which went through his legs for four runs, the crowed booed. As if to hasten the victory, both batsmen, in turn, hit hard and high to the boundary, taking eighteen runs off Ring's final over. Surely we couldn't lose now – there were only fourteen runs required.

Sir Donald Bradman moved into our dressing room, to be the first to congratulate me, but, with ten runs to go, I preferred to wait for the kill, and with the police moving on to the field, Hassett took the ball for what was to be the final over of the match. Three flashing strokes from McLean's bat, the match was over, the rubber saved, and Sir Donald wringing my hand.

Slowly the tension drained away, leaving me almost lightheaded, and as the boys crowded round, and we congratulated one another, I felt a lump in my throat, and my eyes filled with tears. It would not be wrong to say that I was overcome with joy – this match had proved the achievement of an object which Ken Viljoen and I had set out to fulfil as far back as May, 1952. Roy and Headley walked into the dressing room – and I put an arm round both their necks – what a partnership – a great double for Roy, and a magnificent opening to Headley's Test cricket career.

The tumult and the shouting died, and Ken and I sat quietly together in a corner of the dressing room. As I slowly packed my bag, we were far too full for words, but both of us knew what was uppermost in the other's mind – we had kept our faith with the South African Cricket Board; we had answered the critics in full.

On 12th February, 1953 I was on board a cargo ship between Freemantle and Adelaide. I spent most of the day stuck firmly to a wireless in the ship's lounge. When we docked in Adelaide the next morning I rushed off to buy a newspaper. The headlines protested at Geoff Noblet's omission from the test team to tour England. On an inside page I found a tiny article recording bluntly the Sprinbok's victory in the 5th Test at Melbourne – just the bald fact, nothing more. Maybe the Australians don't take kindly to losing cricket tests and would rather not noise such failure abroad.

They were to suffer further at the hands of the Springboks.

NEWLANDS, 1955

Mention the 1955 Lions to people who were around at the time, and their eyes grow misty with delight. And then they'll start muttering some names in a reverent litany – Tony O'Reilly, Cliff Morgan, Butterfield and Davies, Dickie Jeeps ... They were certainly men that set South Africa alight.

Recall the picture of the final act of the first test, played before 96 000 and more spectators at the old Ellis Park. There is Tommy Gentles pushing himself up off the ground as he looks towards the goal posts. There is Ralph Burmeister in white jersey, white shorts and white takkies squatting on his haunches, looking at the posts. And there is the central figure of Jack van der Schyff, head dropped, body hollow as if taking a bullet. He is slumping away from the posts. The ball is travelling past the left hand upright. South Africa lost 23-22 in what is still considered by many as the greatest test of all times.

So much was the drama of that first test at Ellis Park that the greatness of Stephen Fry's Springboks' achievement in the second test at Newlands a fortnight later is often forgotten.

Vivian Jenkins's book on the tour is entitled *The Lions Rampant*. The adjective is apt. When they got to Newlands for the second test they had scored 72 tries in 16 matches, one every 18 playing minutes. Opponents had managed slightly more than one a match.

Reg Sweet in *Pride of the Lions* describes the test:

> For a start, at any rate, there was little hint of the drama that was to overtake this test. Dryburgh went for an angled penalty and missed, Davies slipped through in the centre but Butterfield was well pulled down by Sinclair before the damage became irre-

parable, and then Meredith heeled and held near the Springbok posts. Over-eager flank forwards were trapped off-side by one of the oldest dodges in the scrummager's repertoire for Cameron, with not a problem in the world, to goal at his ease.

Now penalties were missed on either side, at what time certain telling factors had begun to emerge. There was, without a shade of doubt, a more concerted Springbok shove than ever there had been at Ellis Park. It was applied, too, at the moment of the heel whenever the Lions "had the head". And it meant, inevitably, that the ball came tardily to Jeeps, too slowly to Morgan for him to snipe at the defence as he had on the Rand; and appreciably too late to Butterfield and Davies for this admirable centre pair to get fully under way. The Lions, it was clear, had a struggle on their hands.

Moreover, there was no longer the doubt about the centre defence that Ellis Park had raised so often. Rosenberg was here the man on trial, and there were those who had greeted his inclusion with the view that Rosenberg, fine attacking player though he was, had neither the physique nor, to reduce it to the simplest terms, the sheer strength to stand up to forthright tackling, whether on the giving or receiving end.

But Rosenberg it was who came in low and hard, repeatedly and successfully, to halt the strong-striding Davies in his tracks, and at once the question had been answered. In the loose, too, despite the valiant efforts of Greenwood in particular, it was most often Fry, Retief or Ackermann who were quickest upon the open ball and opportunities to strike out from the broken play were being denied the British Isles.

It was just on half-time that the first break-through was made: the forwards ran clear, Fry and Retief prominent as they handled crisply with short passes to carry them beyond the cover; then out to the threes and Sinclair, running hard, kicked across. A spurt of flying feet which was van Vollenhoven, to snatch the ball from the air ahead of three or four defenders, a 25-yard sprint, and he was there for a try that had all the virtues of pace and anticipation.

Now it seemed less important that Dryburgh failed again to goal, for at three-all half the match remained and it was only too apparent that this was a resurgent Springbok side.

Confirmation was not long in coming. Griffiths joined the line on the open side as the second half got under way, but the timing and direction of the final pass to O'Reilly was not calculated to assist and priceless points had been squandered. Then Ulyate retaliated, looking for the opening as Gentles served him. As he grub-kicked through the gap away went van Vollenhoven on the left, and Sinclair in the centre. It was in fact Sinclair who snapped up the ball as he went, and in midfield he was clear.

O'Reilly was faced with an impossible problem. Cameron was late as he hurried across, and O'Reilly alone could possibly deal with Sinclair. Five yards from the line he pulled him down. Greenwood covered fast, but Sinclair had put van Vollenhoven away ... and with Greenwood on his back as they tumbled across the line, van Vollenhoven had put South Africa ahead for the first time in the match. Dryburgh failed to goal from the angle, but the deluge was upon the Lions.

In ten minutes, ten almost unbelievably rousing minutes of thrust upon inspired thrust, three more tries were hurried onto the board and the second test, now and for all time, had been won conclusively. First it was van Vollenhoven again, receiving from Gentles on the blind-side and with no room for manoeuvre on his left. Only an infield swerve was left to him, and swerve he did ... gathering pace as he probed for the opening between O'Reilly and Jeeps, finding it, and racing down upon Cameron, whom he beat completely as he shaped to go outside, swung hard infield in the moment that Cameron was committed, and scored at the posts.

It was as fine a try as the match produced, and van Vollenhoven – the somewhat fortunate van Vollenhoven to be here at all, following his unpromising bow at Ellis Park – had at once become the first South African to score three tries in a test at home, and equalled the record set against Ireland in 1912 by E.E. McHardy and Jan Stegman. Ulyate took the kick this time, with no better fortune.

There were elements in this match which had now begun to resemble that most celebrated day of all, the 44-0 victory over Scotland at Murrayfield. Koch, Fry and du Rand had all played there, among these magnificent forwards. Sinclair and Bekker had seen it too. And the thought no doubt occurred to Cameron, now at full back, who had been at fly-half for Scotland on that extraordinary day.

Hard on the heels of van Vollenhoven's third came Rosenberg's try, made possible by Sinclair as he cut the line between Davies and Butterfield in the centre. He made ground and then sent Rosenberg on his way; and Rosenberg, the new boy making good, threw back his head in the time-honoured manner so familiar for the Transvaal, streaked across the Newlands turf on the angle for the corner, beat what remained of the covering defence and Cameron, whom Sinclair had drawn effectively, and slithered across the line for try number four.

His ambition spurred by this success, Rosenberg now carved out the opening for the fifth try. Dryburgh, alive to the opportunity at full-back, cracked on the pace and linked up on his outside – and so, with a final burst across the line, became the first South African full-back since Percy Allport, on this same ground against Tom Smyth's side of 1910, to score a test match try. For good measure Dryburgh goaled this one, too, and in ten rampaging minutes the Springboks had hastened into a 17-3 lead which looked to be inviolable.

The packed Newlands ground had seldom known such a day as this. It seemed not to be certain whether to sit or to leap up on excited feet; and it settled for round after echoing round of untrammelled applause which must have rolled a long way up the slopes of Devil's Peak behind the towering new stand, and out across the suburbs . . . not that the party was yet at an end.

A Lion's movement broke down going left, and Ulyate darted in to take possession with impressive appreciation of a fleeting chance. Briers, on the right wing, went with him, took the pass and raced across near the corner.

Now a closing flurry of excitement. At last the British backs were in their stride, Morgan going hard before he slipped a pass back to Butterfield with the defence outstripped and a try ready-made which Cameron could not goal. Then South Africa again as Ackermann booted the ball clear from a line-out and chased after it to ground try number seven, though he did appear to have pushed Jeeps out of the way and may have been fortunate to get the benefit of the doubt. Dryburgh kicked the goal. And in the dying minute it was Davies, on a loose ball swiftly for the Lions, who ran strongly to hand on to Greenwood – and the ever-present Bryn Meredith who accepted the final pass to score.

It was a victory of the order normally discribed as "resounding": a triumph for fast, incisive back-play built upon a foundation of admirable and decisive work in the pack, and of supporting play of quite superlative order in which Retief at No. 8, especially, had played notably well.

No Springbok side had ever previously scored seven tries in a home international. For the matter of that, few had ever attacked with such conviction. The rubber had been squared at the halfway mark, and the series of 1955 would assuredly be reckoned among the finest of them all.

THE TEAMS
British Isles – A. Cameron (Scotland); G.M. Griffiths (Wales), W.P.C. Davies (England), J. Butterfield (England), A.J.F.

O'Reilly (Ireland), C.I. Morgan (Wales), R.E.G. Jeeps (Northampton); W.O.G. Williams (Wales), B.V. Meredith (Wales), C.C. Meredith (Wales), J.T. Greenwood (Scotland), R.H. Thompson (Ireland, captain), R.H. Williams (Wales), R.J. Robins (Wales) and T.E. Reid (Ireland).

South Africa – R.G. Dryburgh (Western Province); K.T. van Vollenhoven (Northern Transvaal), D.J. Sinclair (Transvaal), W. Rosenberg (Transvaal), T.P.D. Briers (Western Province); C.A. Ulyate (Transvaal), T.A. Gentles (Western Province); H.J. Bekker (Northern Transvaal), A.J. van der Merwe (Boland), A.C. Koch (Boland), S.P. Fry (Western Province, captain), J.A. du Rand (Northern Transvaal), J.T. Claassen (Western Transvaal), D.S.P. Ackermann (Western Province) and D.F. Retief (Northern Transvaal).

Scorers – Van Vollenhoven (3), Rosenberg, Dryburgh, Briers, Ackermann (tries), Dryburgh (two conversions) for South Africa; Butterfield, B.V. Meredith (tries), Cameron (penalty goal) for British Isles.

Referee – Mr. M. Slabbert. Attendance 46,000.

The seven tries scored by the Springboks that day remains the most tries ever scored against the Lions. When the eyes get misty in recalling the 1955 Lions and the fervour the tour engendered (including death threats against Stephen Fry), it is well to remember that the series was drawn and that the Springboks in fact scored 16 tries, still the highest number for any test series in the history of world rugby and six more than the Lions scored in sharing the series.

TRIUMPH AND TRAGEDY

Gert Potgieter is one of the most glorious of South Africa's sportsmen and yet one of the saddest. A great natural athlete, his level of achievement, apparently with minimum effort, was enormous. And, when that is said, it could have been still greater, far greater.

They nearly did not choose the young policeman in 1958 when South Africa was picking a side to take to the Empire and Commonwealth Games, as they were then called, in Cardiff. Injury had nearly ruled him out anyway. Certainly nobody was ready for what was to come, and it happened almost casually when it did happen.

It would not have happened at all if rugby football had had its way with Gert Potgieter who played centre for Northern Transvaal Under 19 in 1955 and then went on to play for the senior team in 1956 and 1957 when he broke three vertebrae in his neck tackling a heavy forward. He spent six weeks in plaster and could start training only at Christmas time in 1957. The Games would be in July, 1958.

That was only the first setback. At Easter he injured a thigh muscle and missed the trials and nearly missed the Games altogether. His coach, Joe Sirakis recalls:

> The South African Championships in Bloemfontein were only six or seven weeks away when the plaster was removed from his neck. Gert was keen to compete, so we had to rush his training and a time of 51.3 sec was fairly encouraging.
>
> But alas, as luck would have it, Gert pulled a thigh muscle and it had a bad mental effect on him. Psychologically, I was faced with a real poser. Training was cut down to a minimum, as even ordinary calisthenics caused unpleasantness.

138

The upshot was that on the day of the Empire Games trials in Durban 'Pottie' was in no condition to run the 440 yards hurdles, and everyone was shocked at his non-participation. It was the same for the national championships at Bloemfontein. He could have made the attempt, but, mentally, was not quite ready. Physiotherapy and easy jogging became the daily routine.

When it came to the selection of the Springbok team, Potgieter was nominated on condition that he proved himself worthy of selection in a trial run before the team left for Cardiff. A week before the scheduled departure date he ran an official time trial over the 440 yards flat, clocking 48.0 sec. – which surely provided some proof of his fitness. The Press, however, did not seem completely satisfied with this performance, taking the line that this qualified him only to run in a relay event!

So officialdom demanded that he be tried over the full 440 yards hurdles two days before departure. It must be appreciated that Gert, at the time, suffered immense strain psychologically, mentally and physically to satisfy the exacting demands of those in authority.

Gert was worrying over all the Press ballyhoo and was beginning to see the 440 yards hurdles as a real hoodoo. So, four days before D Day, we decided to hold a very secret test run. He faced the ten obstacles with understandable misgivings, but a slow run over the first two hurdles seemed to settle his nerves to some extent, and then we saw the determination and self-confidence he so often displayed when the odds were against him. Moving into his usual rhythmical, effortless striding with a noticeable increase in speed over the last hurdle, he clocked 51.8 sec. unpaced. Not bad for a much-criticised athlete!

A pointer to what was to follow in the Games at Cardiff was provided when, two days before, Gert had a training run of two miles in the morning and in the afternoon two 440 yards repetition runs, the first in 50.3 sec. and the second – after a 10-minute rest – in

49.2 sec. This convinced Ray Czisek, the American coach, that there was nothing wrong with Gert's physical condition and that he would do well.

Gert Potgieter had been to the Olympic Games in 1956 in Melbourne, when he was nineteen and he may well have won a bronze medal behind Glenn Davis and Eddie Southern of America had he not stumbled and fallen at the final hurdle to end sixth in the final in 56 secs.

Joe Sirakis first met Gert Potgieter at the Police College in Pretoria when Gert Potgieter, from Vryheid in Northern Natal, first came to the College. The college held its athletic trials and nobody could overlook Gert Potgieter.

Gert, in a matter of half-an-hour, did the following: He ran 100 yards in a cool 9.9 sec., long-jumped 23ft., triple-jumped 47ft. and then spotted the half-milers getting ready, so joined them. He took the lead, setting a hot pace until just past the 660 yd. mark when the effort taxed his strength and he had to slow down but still ran the distance in 1 min. 59 sec.!

Hurdles were to bring him fame and glory, and that defeat in Melbourne helped. Because he had fallen in Melbourne, he decided to develop the ability to lead with either leg. Normally it was the left but soon the right was just as proficient with the result that he was taking fourteen strides between hurdles to the fifteen of Glenn Davis and other 440-yard hurdlers. It meant that he could adapt easily to any change of pace or hurdle clearance.

To be fair to a man often accused of being lazy and reliant just on natural ability, Gert Potgieter practised hard to make hurdling a natural movement. He also worked hard on fitness because the quarter-mile was a hard race enough without throwing in ten hurdles along the way.

Potgieter went to Cardiff via Germany. At Duisberg he did 51.3 for the 440 yards hurdles and at Cologne 50 seconds dead. The world record was 49.9, set by Glenn Davis in June, 1958.

The Duke of Edinburgh opened the Empire Games in Cardiff on 18th July, 1958, a Friday. The oath taken read:

'We declare that we shall take part in the true spirit of sportsmanship for the honour of our Commonwealth and for the glory of sport.'

Gert Potgieter would be in action that very first day and he broke the Empire record in his heat – 51.9. Closest to him was David Lean of Australia with 52 secs followed by B Rotich of Kenya (52.8) and GA Shephard of Canada (53.3). It looked as if South Africa had a winner.

At the Empire Games, South Africa expected to have winners, and there were gold medals in Cardiff that year – Reg Gaffley, the bantamweight weight-lifter, Fanie du Plessis for discus, three for bowls, five for boxing, and four for wrestling amongst them at this, South Africa's last appearance at the Empire Games. Fanie du Plessis broke the Empire discus record and Malcolm Spence, like Potgieter, broke the 440 yards record in the heats.

On July, 21st, a week before Prince Charles was created Prince of Wales, Gert Potgieter won his heat in the semi-final and again he broke the Empire record, this time in 51.1 s on a hot day. The final would be the next day.

There were 32 000 people, the biggest crowd of the Games, in the stadium that Tuesday afternoon, and twice within half an hour the South African flag was raised on the victory mast, first for Fanie du Plessis.

Gert Potgieter was in Lane 5, David Lean, who had won the title in 1954, in Lane 6. It was cold and a 14-mile-an-hour wind swirled around the track and would hit the athletes down the back straight.

Lean made the running, and Potgieter had only one ambition – to beat him. Potgieter took a clear lead at the halfway mark, running with 'ease, grace and nonchalance', as John Pitts, who was there, described it. As he came into the home straight he looked back, while his mother, Kitty Potgieter, in Vryheid prayed that he would not look back because 'it is a bad habit he has'. He looked back to see where Lean was and then cruised on to the finish, winning by six yards from Lane with Rotich of Kenya in third place. Joe Sirakis described his protege's run as 'a fairly well-judged race, not bad for an athlete who nearly didn't make the team'.

The crowd were less given to understatement as they rose to the winner and his time – 49.7 secs, 0.2 secs faster than the world record of Glenn Davis. It was a new world record.

The news reached Vryheid and the whole Potgieter family rejoiced. Father Chris was too overwhelmed to speak, and mother first wanted to sing a psalm and then expressed her fears at her son's bachelor status, 'because every girl in Vryheid now wants to hug and kiss him – and that goes for me too. And I don't want to lose my boy yet'. Her prayers were answered, but it was close.

Gert was as modest in success as one could wish an athlete to be. 'David Lean put up a terrific pace, which helped me to break the record. I must pay tribute to our American coach, Ray Czisek. He has the right approach when developing one's mental attitude before a big race. The Welsh provided a track conducive to fast times.' And then he added, 'If my times continue to compare with those of the best Russian and American athletes, I will go on running. Otherwise I will go back to rugby.'

Gert Potgieter, of the broken neck, did not go back to rugby. His times continued to outstrip the best Russian and American athletes, but the irony of it all was that, although he was immaculately prepared for the Olympic Games in Rome in 1960, he did not take part at all.

In 1959 Gert Potgieter won the 440 yards hurdles at the World Games in Helsinki. In one of his closest races he beat Howard of America by only two yards.

On 23rd April, 1960 Gert Potgieter turned 23 and he gave himself a birthday present which only he could manufacture – a world record in the 440 yards hurdles of 49.3, clipping 0.4 secs off his own record, even though he was so nervous that they had to hold up the start while he rid himself of nausea and even though he had forgotten his starting blocks in his anxiety. The principle cause of his anxiety was his doubt whether he could beat Peter Thorburn!

Joe Sirakis and Gert Potgieter worked on all aspects of running – speed, stamina, strength, suppleness. Pottie changed the setting of his starting blocks half-a-dozen times in one session and practised some 40 starts before he decided that he was satisfied with the original setting. He was peaking for the Games, and so was Glenn Davis of the USA, determined to be the top man again.

As a warm-up, Gert Potgieter went to West Germany to take part, gently, in some meetings there. In the small hours of the morning Gert Potgieter was a passenger in a car coming back from an athletic-function. 'Judge' Jeffries was driving and Gert Wolmarans of *Die Vaderland* was on his left. Gert was behind Jeffries and next to him was an attractive German athlete, Renate Junker who now lives in South Africa as Renate Potgieter.

They were talking about athletics, and Gert Potgieter was saying that he would be willing to give up the 400m hurdles if it would help the South African team win the 400m relay.

The car skidded on a bend and hit a tree. John Pitts saw Gert Potgieter in a hospital in Heidelberg and did not expect him to live. An operation was performed, lasting nearly three hours. His jaw was broken, the left side of his face badly lacerated, and his left eye blinded. Gert Potgieter missed the Olympics, and Glenn Davis won the 400m hurdles in 49.3 secs. He ran again but without the will to do really well. ('The big difference was that with more training I did not get the results I used to with more effort'), became an athletics coach, and did not add to the six caps which he had as a centre for Northern Transvaal.

AC Parker, sportswriter over many, many years, has this to say: 'Of all the top sportsmen I've known, Gerhardus Cornelius Potgieter ranks as my most unforgettable character.'

POLLOCK AND BARLOW

The South African cricket side of the Sixties and the early Seventies was the greatest this country has ever produced. Sadly it went largely unknown entirely because of the intransigence of the South African government which sent its ugly, rasping message clearly to the world when BJ Vorster, the prime minister followed HF Verwoerd's example of stopping Maori All Blacks from coming to South Africa, by telling England that Basil D'Oliviera could not tour with the MCC while thousands of others in Bloemfontein cheered. The irony of it all is that the South African government would later spend millions to bring black cricketers to this country. In the meantime the greatest generation of all South African cricketers played very few tests indeed. But the few that they did play were magic. At no other time have South African cricketers produced such panache, excitement, confidence and athletism.

It all started with a humble tour in 1963, the second children's crusade. Jack Cheetham had taken a team of unknowns to Australia in 1952 and they had come back with glory. This time it was Trevor Goddard's turn to lead them with Ken Viljoen, manager of Cheetham's side, again the Springbok manager. The only other player with experience was John Waite.

The rest of the team (ages in brackets) was: Eddie Barlow (23), Clive Halse (28 but on his first international cricketing outing), Kelly Seymour (27), Peter Pollock (22), Colin Bland (25), Graeme Pollock (19), Denis Lindsay (24), David Pithey (27), Tony Pithey (30), Joe Partridge (31), Peter van der Merwe (26), Buster Farrer (27), and Peter Carlstein (25). Only the following in the team had had test match experience:

Goddard, Waite, Peter Pollock, Tony Pithey, Farrer and Carlstein.

Players who had played against New Zealand the previous season and were not on this trip included Jackie McGlew, Roy McClean, Sid O'Linn, Kim Elgie, Goofy Lawrence, Kenny Walter, Tiger Lance, Syd Burke, Harry Bromfield, Peter Heine, and Neil Adcock. As in 1952, though not quite as impressively, Australian cricket had many giants – Brian Booth, Richie Benaud, Bill Lawry, Bobby Simpson, Wally Grout, and 'the new Bradman' in Norman O'Neill.

The tour started effectively with a win over Western Australia in Perth and then there was the surest sign of things to come in a drawn match with a Combined XI – a double century from Barlow and 127 not out from Graeme Pollock, when the Springboks scored 532/3 in their second innings. Defeat in the next match at Adelaide was followed by a remarkable victory – by an innings and 101 runs over New South Wales at Sydney Cricket Ground.

Things were not quite as good after that as Queensland thrashed the Springboks and the first test in Brisbane ended in a draw – but not a dull draw as controversy arose, luckily not caused by the South Africans.

Picked for Australia was Ian Meckiff who had a reputation as a chucker. The main interest before the test was centred on possible action against him by the umpires. The spectators were not disappointed.

Australia batted first and made 435 with Booth 169, O'Neill 82 and Peter Pollock 6/95. Ian Meckiff took the ball for the second Australian over. The square leg umpire was Colin Egar, a friend of Meckiff's and the umpire who had been at Wes Hall's end in the tied test with the West Indies.

Meckiff bowled, and the ball went through to Grout. Meckiff went back and came in for the second ball. 'No ball!', called Egar, and everybody knew what it was for. Next ball and Egar shouted again. Two balls later again and again on the ninth ball, and Ian Meckiff had bowled his last over in test cricket after 18 tests and 45 wickets including 9/107 against England at Melbourne, a sad end for the likeable left-hander. Strange that, as in the case of Griffin in 1960, they had to use the test arena to rid cricket of a chucker.

Rain put the test out of its misery, and although Eddie Barlow scored his first test hundred, the match remained the Meckiff affair. There were all sorts of threats and acrimony flying around a country not known for beating about the bush.

Melbourne had been good to Cheetham's Springboks but it gave Goddard's a rough hiding by 8 wickets when Bobby Simpson took over the captaincy from an injured Benaud, who strangely had taken the brunt of public ire for not switching Meckiff to the other end to see if Lou Rowan's view differed from that of Colin Egar.

There was no Meckiff but there was controversy. Trial by television proved that Bill Lawry was out hit wicket when he had 4. Lou Rowan did not see it and Lawry kept quiet about it and went on to make 157, a significant contribution to Australia's victory.

Barlow got another century and for the only time in test cricket there were two sets of brothers in one side – the Pitheys and the Pollocks.

A week later they were up in Sydney for the third test. Benaud was back in the side but Simpson retained the captaincy. Goddard lost the third toss in a row and the Aussies batted.

The Springbok attack depended on Peter Pollock and Joe Partridge who died so tragically in Zimbabwe in 1988, and Pollock was so injured that the doctor had said that he would not play for three weeks. The Springboks took a chance and Pollock played. Australia were all out 260 – Pollock 5/83, Partridge 4/88.

The Springboks bettered that, and Graeme Pollock scored his first test century – 122 in 3 hours and 40 minutes. In that time the Springboks scored 186 runs. Graeme Pollock says, 'I like to recall my second fifty best because I felt on top of the world and I think it showed in my strokes. For once none of the bowling seemed difficult, not even that of Benaud, Mc-Kenzie and Hawke whom most people would rate as the world's best in their different styles. I believe I reached this fifty with seventeen scoring shots.'

It was Graeme Pollock's second century on the Sydney Cricket Ground, hill and all. Lindsay Hasset said, 'I never have heard a sweeter note than the one young Graeme Pollock brought to Australia in his bat.' And Hasset had played with Bradman. Dick Whitington wrote, 'It was this century of young Pollock's in my opinion, that turned the whole trend of the series, and possibly changed the whole character of South African batsmanship.'

The rest of the Springboks were skittled and the lead was only 42 when the Aussies went in, and they made merry, declaring at 450/9. Simpson's declaration left them 409 runs to get in 433 minutes but they were unwilling to take the risk of going 2-0 down in the series, ending with 326/5.

There was another match at Melbourne Cricket Ground before the next test, against Victoria, and again Pollock and Barlow got runs. Pollock and Goddard put on 203 in 166 minutes of which Pollock scored 110, but again there was a draw as the Victorians bashed the ball all over the place in their second innings chase for runs. But now Adelaide beckoned and the fourth test.

The following accounts are taken from the Pollock brothers, Peter in his book *The Thirty Tests,* Graeme in *Down the Wicket:*

> *Peter:* What happened in the fourth test at Adelaide should be recorded in letters of gold – rather green and gold. This was the triumph of all triumphs.
>
> Who will forget that victory celebration, that party around the motel swimming pool with all the champagne at the bottom of the deep end and Colin Bland insisting that "if you want to drink you'll have to dive for it"?
>
> Who will forget Trevor Goddard, the teetotaller with the giggles after a glass of champagne? Yes, who could possibly forget the realisation of a dream? At some stages it might have appeared to be an "impossible dream" but as Eddie Barlow always said "Nothing is impossible if you believe you can do it".
>
> *Graeme:* As a country I liked Australia very much. I liked the climate, the scenery, and the motels in which

we were accommodated. Out-of-the-way, these motels are well equipped with a swimming pool, television, and large bedrooms with private baths. We shared a room with a different team-mate each time. This conforms to the South African idea on tour of avoiding cliques and promoting good team spirit, and works well.

I liked the Australian people – even the barrackers, who are so much part of the game 'Down Under'. At least they show a keen interest in what is going on; they don't just sit there. I also thought the press boys treated us well, and reported the games fairly.

I liked the beaches, and the golf courses – though the latter had me struggling a bit in such expert company as that of Johnny Waite and Buster Farrer. I enjoyed the odd game of tennis, particularly partnering Peter Carlstein to beat Richie Benaud and 'Slasher' Ken Mackay.

I liked the cities, the well-equipped cricket grounds and wickets which help the man who is prepared to play strokes while still giving the bowler a chance. And though less spectacular than Sydney or Melbourne I liked Adelaide, best of all.

Mind you, I am prejudiced, because it was in the Fourth Test in lovely hot weather at pretty Adelaide that South Africa finally hit dazzling form to enjoy the highspot of our tour.

Peter: It started with a hassle. Johnny Waite wasn't fit and only minutes before the toss he decided to stand down. In came Denis Lindsay vowing that Johnny would never get his wicket-keeping berth back. We lost the toss for the fourth time in a row, but round one went to me. I had had an altercation with Norman O'Neill at Sydney. Once the wicket had flattened out in the Sydney match Norman was full of back-chat describing my bouncers as "cream-puffs".

Well, I struck early that morning at Adelaide getting Bill Lawry. In came Norman O'Neill and six balls later he was back in the "hut" with a duck. In attempting to fend off a bouncer he nudged the ball into Trevor Goddard's hands in the gully.

"You can't handle cream-puffs", I shouted as I marched triumphantly down the wicket. Yes, the action was on. Bobby Simpson, Peter Burge, Brian Booth and Barry Shepherd all played extremely well but as seemed to be the case with the Australian batsmen in the series, they inexplicably got out when centuries were in sight. Thank heavens, anyway. The Aussies totalled 345 with Trevor Goddard being rewarded for his nagging accuracy with a bag of five wickets.

Out went Goddard and Barlow and as they did so regularly in this series, they got us off to a comfortable start. Trevor nudging them here and there, Barlow whacking the odd boundary. The score mounted and reached 70. Then came the crisis and the turning point.

The bowler was Neil Hawke, whose action is anything but textbook but who moves the ball around quite disconcertingly. He started the over by clean bowling Goddard and then back went Tony Pithey, second ball. Seventy for two wasn't looking so good. In strode Graeme Pollock.

The first two balls beat him all ends up.

The next ball Graeme met with the full face of the bat and sent it scurrying into the covers. It was an effortless shot but the ball seemed to gain momentum as it sped into the pickets. And this was to be the pattern for the next four hours and forty minutes of play. Barlow and Pollock took complete control. They massacred the Australian bowling in a display of ruthless authority that would have made even Hitler look like a weak-kneed diplomat. The song that Barlow and Pollock sang was so sweet that even the most ardent Australian supporter couldn't begrudge the sheer magnificence of it all.

Theirs was a double-barrelled assault. They were like two matadors out for the kill together, and they accomplished their brutal task with poise and grace.

Eddie Barlow stepping out of his crease to smash a

Benaud "flipper" through the covers looked like daddy playing with junior on the back lawn. Graeme's bat spoke with an eloquence of its own.

Eddie finished with a brilliant double century and Graeme eventually succumbed to the wiles of bowler Hawke for 175. But they had compiled a mammoth 337 runs in their glorious batting duet.

Bill O'Reilly, Australia's greatest bowler of any era and at that time doyen of cricket writers Down Under, stood hatless in the pressbox to applaud as Graeme – the first to go – left the arena. It is not customary for cricket writers to clap their hands in applause but O'Reilly couldn't let an occasion like this go by without showing emotion and appreciation. Without wishing to detract from Eddie's innings, there is little doubt that the role of "Prince Charming" belonged to Graeme. His innings was compiled with a laconic mastery almost incongruous and quite unbelievable from one so young and innocent of countenance.

An indelible chapter had been written into cricket history by these two fairhaired Springboks. Records tumbled and so too did the reputations of the Australian bowlers. The Springboks finished with 595.

Graeme: Eddie Barlow had a really golden trip. He was making runs nearly every innings, and when he wasn't he was taking catches or bowling out the opposition. At Adelaide he just couldn't go wrong. The longer he stayed at the wicket the more confident he became, the more he chanced-his-arm and the more fantastic were his shots.

Richie Benaud, who played in this Test under Simpson's captaincy, is a very crafty bowler. He is without doubt the best leg-spinner I have ever played against, or am ever likely to play against. Yet Eddie treated him with the utmost contempt. He would move a foot outside his leg stump and cut him hard off the back foot, clipping the ball almost off his bails. The nerve of it! Since that day Eddie has always believed: 'When in trouble, lie back and cut.'

Peter: A first innings lead of 250 was all the inspiration the Springbok bowlers needed. The Aussies didn't give up easily – they never do – but the leeway was too much. However, by late afternoon on the fourth day a spirited sixth wicket partnership between Richie Benaud and Barry Shepherd was starting to cause a little consternation. Everything had been thrown at them but they were going along a little too nicely. Came five o'clock, an hour to close and Eddie Barlow went up to the skipper.

Graeme: Things were getting a bit out of control when Eddie Barlow asked Trevor Goddard to put him on to bowl. 'I've had a premonition. I'm sure I can get these fellows out,' Eddie told the skipper. For some time Trevor preferred to rely on his more regular bowlers to make the breakthrough, but Eddie kept pestering him. Eventually Eddie told the skipper: 'Look here, you'd better put me on in the next over or so or I'm going to lose this premonition.' At that point, more out of desperation than free choice (I imagine) Trevor relented, and handed the ball to the ebullient Barlow.

Peter: In his very first over Eddie sent down a long-hop and Shepherd, going for the hook, mistimed his shot and sent the ball skywards in the general direction of fine leg. Denis Lindsay, pads and all, realising that the ball wasn't going to carry to me at fine-leg, set off and a full length dive climaxed a miraculous catch.

But this was not to be the end of Eddie's contribution. A couple of balls later Richie dragged one from outside the off-stump onto his wickets. In came McKenzie. Eddie accidentally – though he insists otherwise – let go a full toss which Garth hit in the meat but straight back at Eddie.

"Bunter" relished the offering and in the space of a few minutes had changed the whole complexion of the Australian fight-back. It just goes to show what can be achieved when you are a "believer" like Eddie Barlow.

Graeme: In his spell of five overs Eddie took 3 vital wickets for 6 runs, and the match was virtually sewn up in our favour. It wasn't so much a case of brilliant bowling – I've seen him bowl much better than this – but of a chap in the middle of a purple patch in which he could do no wrong. His premonition certainly paid off – and no wonder we dubbed him 'Superman'.

Australia lost their last four wickets in the last 30 minutes of the fourth day, and on the morning of the final day Trevor Goddard and Barlow (naturally) had no trouble in scoring the 82 runs we needed for a ten-wicket triumph.

Just a few statistics may put into perspective the greatness of the Barlow-Pollock partnership. They scored their 341 runs in 283 minutes. It is the highest partnership in South African test history. Graeme Pollock hit three sixes and 18 fours, Barlow 27 fours. Pollock took 31 runs off two overs from Bobby Simpson who ended with 0/59 while Richie Benaud, the other leg spinner, ended with 0/101.

After Hannibal had thrashed the Romans at Cannae, his brother accused him of knowing how to win a battle but not a war. The Springboks had passed up a chance of victory in the third test. They threw away their chance of winning the series in the fifth test, partly through a surprising lack of belief in themselves after the glories of Adelaide.

The fifth test was at Sydney Cricket Ground, and for the first time in the series Goddard won the toss. He put Australia in. Joe Partridge swung it all over the place, taking 7/91, and the Australians were out for 311. Partridge liked the Sydney Cricket Ground. Colin Bland was the best of the Springbok batsmen and although they gained a lead of 100 runs, they did so slowly. Time was to win the test.

The Australians tumbled to 245/9 with about three hours left when Tom Veivers and Neil Hawke put on 45 runs in 80 minutes to leave the Springboks to score 171 at two runs a minute and Graeme Pollock nursing a broken finger. The result was a draw and the series was a draw with the Springboks clearly the better side.

The Second Children's Crusade had been a success.

THE PAIN AND THE GLORY

It's a story every rugby playing boy should know. It is the stuff that boyhood dreams and heroes are made of, containing as it does the essence of all those boys' paper stories. Success snatched from disaster through the happy coincidence of skill and physical courage on the part of the dashingly handsome hero. There is a difference though – this story is true.

In 1964 Western Province went to play Northern Transvaal at Loftus Versfeld, a journey of humiliation, so it seemed.

A month before Western Province had been there for a "friendly" – if such a thing is possible between two such uncompromising rivals – and been thrashed 25-9. The Saturday before this second clash South Africa had lost to France in the scruffiest of all test matches at Springs, and that day there had been seven Western Province players in the Springbok team to the three of Northern Transvaal. And the unhappy northerners blamed two players above all – Mike Lawless and Jannie Engelbrecht, both of Western Province.

The match played at Loftus Versfeld would be no friendly. Emotions were running high as the Northern Tranvaalers prepared to annihilate the rugby snobs from the Western Cape. Secondly, it was a Currie Cup match.

The last time there had been competition for the Currie Cup was in 1959, but the mystique of winning the trophy was far from forgotten or obsolete. The S.A. Rugby Board has tampered with the form of the trophy regularly, and in 1964 it came up with as complicated a scheme as was possible – the division of the fifteen unions then in existene into five sections, the winners of which would play in a league for the trophy without the climax of a final as is the case today. But to all intents and purposes the match between Western Province and Northern Transvaal was the final, certainly the decider.

It had not been a smooth year for Doug Hopwood's Western Province team, starting as it did with a draw with South Western Districts at Oudtshoorn. To make matters worse John Gainsford had been crocked in the test with the French the Saturday before and would miss the match, Wynand Mans joining Dave Stewart in the centre.

Doug Hopwood gave his team the shortest possible team talk in the Union Hotel before they set off for the ground: "Chaps, we haven't done much this season. Let's give it a full go today."

They did, but the possibility of disaster seemed confirmed as the match progressed. The central figure in it all was Jannie Engelbrecht, first, apparently, as a disaster victim, then finally as the hero. Many a coach and many a father would tell youthful listeners of the glory and heroism of Jannie Engelbrecht on that day.

Before the match Engelbrecht was the target for much vilification in and around Pretoria. They said he was there just to make up the numbers required for a team and that local boy, Ernest du Plessis, would make him look silly. Such was the wrath directed at him that there was even the suggestion that he would be deliberately injured. Like Morné du Plessis a few years later, Jannie Engelbrecht would shut up all those who doubted his courage and skill.

Doug Hopwood says, "All the newspapers were rubbing their hands, saying we were mincemeat. They went through our team, especially the Springboks, saying we were no good or over the wall."

Jannie Engelbrecht says, "There is no doubt that the tension before this game was worse than any I ever felt before a test match." The player had been personally got at, not pleasant in any sport.

There were 37 000 people at Loftus Versfeld, not as commodious a ground in those days, in anticipation of Northern Transvaal glory and vengeance. Their team would set the record straight. The ingredients were there to make an even hotter dish than was normal when north met south, young bulls had a go at the old elite, the right wing met the traditional liberals, and all the other cultural differences that separated the harsh but rich new land from the gentile south.

Half way through the first half an incident occurred which suggested that the prophecy of deliberate injury had come true. But that's jumping the gun somewhat.

Northern Transvaal were immediately on the attack and could have scored in the third minute when Rooies van Wyk late-tackled their fly half, André van Tonder, but Grundlingh missed the kick. Two minutes later they did go ahead when Tiny Neethling, recently moved from lock to prop, was penalised at a line-out. This time Martin Grundlingh made no mistake.

Play seesawed after that but mostly Northern Transvaal were having the more impressive ride. In the 18th minute they wheeled a scrum on the Western Province line and Stompie van der Merwe, the lock who had a great game that day and who died in 1988, scored. 6-0 to Northern Transvaal.

Then disaster struck Western Province. Let Chris Greyvenstein describe it:

> With the score 6-3, the ball was kicked in his direction and it was rolling over the touchline. Engelbrecht followed it and was outside the playing area and bending to pick it up when there was a kaleidoscope of bright, darting, lights in front of his eyes as over 100 kg of muscle and bone hit him from behind and crushed him shoulder-first into the ground.
>
> He felt the collar-bone crack and his agonised mind flashed back to that time before when the same thing had happened and he had to spend two pain-racked nights sitting up on a chair.
>
> Louis Schmidt, captain of Northern Transvaal and at the time the beloved "Bull of the North" with his bristling moustache, had tackled him and it looked as if the critics were right and he would not see out the game.
>
> There were angry words around him as he stood there holding his numbed arm. Johan Fechter, playing on the wing for Northern Transvaal but an old friend from Stellenbosch days, had come over and there was

sympathy and other emotions naked in his eyes. He was waved away and now Hopwood was staring hard into Engelbrecht's face and his urgent voice commanded:

"You're not going off, Jannie. We can't lose you now!"

So the game continued and he found that although he could not lift his injured arm he could control the ball if it was thrown at his midriff.

Half-time came and the team clustered around him. The pain was excruciating and he wanted to go to the dressingroom to have the shoulder strapped up but with the flash of inspiration that comes only to the greatest captains, Hopwood summed up his character and the state of the game with one curt command: "Don't go, Jan. Don't show them anything."

In those days there were no replacements. But the majestic wing was in agony.

Play surged up and down the field. Dave Stewart missed a penalty, Wynand Mans broke, Tiny Naude missed a penalty, Hopwood was doing well at the back of the line-out, and then in the 32nd minute Dave Stewart landed a penalty when Stompie van der Merwe went off-side. 6-3.

Although Grundlingh missed a penalty and Mof Myburgh led a charge, the score was still 6-3 at half-time.

Eight minutes into the second half Jannie Engelbrecht ran himself into history. Northern Transvaal moved the ball down the line, but the movement broke down at outside centre. Wynand Mans picked up and passed to Gert Brynard who was covering from the left wing. Nippy Brynard stepped out of a tackle and was off down the field in counter-attack. He ran to Martin Grundlingh, drew him, and carefully, oh so carefully, delicately and sympathetically, he passed to Jannie Engelbrecht running on his outside with his right arm dangling.

It was his right collarbone which had been broken. The ball would be coming from his left, and use of his right hand was vital. Despite the screaming agony – and Jannie who was often injured on the rugby field says that there is no pain to equal the pain of a broken collarbone – Jannie Engelbrecht managed to push his right hand forward into the path of the ball and folded his left around it and draw it up into the crook of his left arm, as he slashed away to score at the poles. Getting it down was complicated and painful but in the speed of the movement he had left the Northern Transvalers stranded and so had time. He lowered himself down onto his side and eased the ball to the ground.

It was a try. Dave Stewart's conversion put Western Province into the lead for the first time.

For the next ten minutes Western Province pressed, missing a penalty and a try when Charlie Cockrell dropped an inside pass from Hopwood close to the Northern Transvaal line.

Then Northern Transvaal came surging back. Martin Grundlingh missed a penalty and Wynand Mans drove them back with an enormous drop out. Then Lawless dropped a pass and Fourie du Preez pounced. Western Province stopped Johan Fechter on the line.

Dennis de Klerk chipped over the Western Province line and a diving Lionel Wilson just got there before a diving Stompie van der Merwe. Martin Grundlingh collected his own kick and the Northern Transvaal forwards drove at the line where Haas Schoeman performed valliant feats. Frik du Preez bullocked for the line and was held up short. Northern Transvaal pushed over the Western Province line and claimed a try. But Fourie du Preez had not got the ball down as Haas Schoeman had got his body between the ball and the ground.

Pressure told. At a line-out 30 yards or so from the Western Province line Stompie van der Merwe fed Dennis de Klerk who slung out a pass to van Tonder, who dropped for goal. It flew high and true, and Northern Transvaal were in the lead. Western Province spirits flagged.

Northern Transvaal were in the lead still in the 38th minute of the second half. There were two minutes and injury time left.

Doug Hopwood remembers the situation and the troublesome scrum half, Dirk de Vos. "Now Dirkie de Vos kept passing the ball Jannie's way, and Jannie came over and said he was going off. I said, 'Stay on. I'll talk to Dirkie.' I went over to Dirkie and said, 'Dirkie, for crying out loud, don't pass to Jannie.' We just wanted Jannie to stay on the field because to take a man out of a pack would have been hopeless. And Dirkie just said, 'Ja,' as he always did. But he never listened."

Chris Greyvenstein:

There was a scrum 10 metres or so from the Western Province line. Dirkie Vos made sure that he caught Jannie's eye and there was a world of meaning in that look that passed between the two of them. He was trying to tell Engelbrecht something and the wing understood the message.

Charlie Cockrell hooked and, pounding like a cat, De Vos scooped up the ball and in a flash had broken past the blindside of the scrum. He eluded flanker Schmidt's despairing grab by hollowing his back and a split second later the quick-silver little scrumhalf had driven the breach he wanted. With nearly 60 metres to go to the corner-flag, De Vos gave Engelbrecht a perfect pass.

There was the pounding of feet behind him and from the corner of his eye he saw Ernest du Plessis straining to cut him off. From somewhere, somehow, came the power to thrust himself away from his opponent and he felt the fingertips brushing his back as he surged along the touchline. Jannie Engelbrecht was keeping date with destiny and nothing could stop him until he finally collapsed over the tryline, hugging that precious ball, and knowing that the game was won.

Hopwood watched from behind. "I had told Dirkie not to pass to Jannie but he didn't listen. He passed to Jannie. When Jannie ran over the try line, he couldn't press the ball down. He had the ball under his broken collarbone and he couldn't get the ball down. He just slid down and fell on it. That was an unbelievable try. It won us the Currie Cup."

Northern Transvaal got onto the attack, and Frik du Preez and Grundlingh tried drop goals but failed. Doug Hopwood took the second drop and hoofed the ball down into the Northern Transvaal 25. At a ruck on the Northern Transvaal line Gerrie Bester passed back to Dennis de Klerk, who fumbled. Rooies van Wyk pounced and scored. Dave Stewart converted, and Captain Kolesky blew the final whistle.

The crowd applauded; some cheered. Hennie Muller ran to his players.

Later that evening Jannie Engelbrecht got to the hospital, where he was x-rayed. The collarbone was broken and his arm was put in a sling. He could hardly move for the pain, but, happily, it, along with all his other rugby injuries, was to have no lasting effect. The knowledge that you are brave probably does have a lasting effect.

Teams:

Western Province: Lionel Wilson; Gert Brynard, Dave Stewart, Wynand Mans, Jannie Engelbrecht; Mike Lawless, Dirk de Vos; Tiny Neethling, Charlie Cockrell, Gert Kotze; Haas Schoeman, Tiny Naude, Andrew Janson, Rooies van Wyk; Doug Hopwood.

Northern Transvaal: Martin Grundlingh; Ernest du Plessis, Gerrie Bester, Elandré de Coning, Johan Fechter; André van Tonder, Dennis de Klerk; Mof Myburgh, Gys Pitzer, Hennie Pretorius; Frik du Preez, Stompie van der Merwe, Jumbo van der Walt, Louis Schmidt; Fourie du Preez.

Referee: Captain Wessel Kolesky.

Northern Transvaal don't lose easily. It was Louis Schmidt's last match for his province. Mind you, he had asked for it, behaving like the king of the kids, taking penalties, kick-offs and drop-outs which usually went straight to Lionel Wilson who would send the ball spinning into touch.

The only member of the Western Province team never to wear a Springbok jersey was Rooies van Wyk whereas the only Springboks on the Northern Transvaal side were Mof Myburgh, Frik du Preez, Gys Pitzer, Stompie van der Merwe, and Louis Schmidt.

SEVEN DOWN AND SEVENTEEN TO PLAY

Seven down and seventeen to play. A hopeless situation? Not for Gary Player the man who was and in fact still is, the epitome of what positive thinking really means.

So often in top sports South Africans as individuals have promised so much only to fall at the last hurdle, the one that really counts. Not so Gary Player. Above all Gary Player. Above all that day at Wentworth in the autumn of 1956 when his opponent was American Tony Lema.

It wasn't the final and it wasn't the victory which Gary Player himself reckons was his greatest. But for many it was the most dramatic of all the great golfer's victories. It was a victory which made South Africans walk tall, as they had done when Karen Muir broke a world record in Blackpool and the Springboks had won at Trent Bridge. It was some consolation for the shocking rugby results first on the short tour of Scotland and Ireland and them on the long tour of Australia and New Zealand. Just when things looked blackest along came Gary Player. Love him or not, Gary Player was a hero. Regard him as sententious or not, he was a wholesome hero.

They say he fell in love with Vivienne Verwey and then only with golf. Vivienne, daughter of Jock Verwey and brother of Bobby, could, so they say, hit a ball far further than the little King Edward's boy, and he was determined not to be outdone. Even after he had married Vivienne he was determined not to be outdone. And even after he had made his millions as one of golf's all time greats he was still determined not to be outdone.

In 1965 Gary Player beat Ken Nagle in a play-off to win the US Open and he then handed back the winning cheque to be used for cancer research, an action which did not find universal approval as people liked to mock Gary Player's seriousness and even his religious convictions. Peter Thompson called him emotionally unstable and a soul-searching hand-wringer.

Handsome Tony Lema was also going well at the time. He had won the British Open in 1964 at the first attempt and the Carling World Championship in 1965.

The two met at Wentworth in the Picadilly Matchplay, the second Picadilly Matchplay, the brainchild of Mark McCormack, the golf promoter, and sponsored by the tobacco company. The Picadilly Matchplay would made the West course at Wentworth, unaffectionately known as the Burma Road because it is one of the world's toughest courses, perhaps the best known course in Britain because of its regular television appearances. All that started in 1965, and it started with Gary Player.

The contestants in 1965 – and they were there by invitation as the greatest achievers in the golfing world – were Tony Lema, Gary Player, Peter Thompson who had won the British Open in 1965, Kel Nagle, Arnie Palmer who had won the first Picadilly, Neil Coles, Christy O'Connor, and Peter Alliss.

There were four 36-hole matches which led to semi-finals, one between Arnie Palmer and Peter Thompson, the other between Gary Player and Tony Lema. Player had beaten Coles, Lema Alliss, both without difficulty.

Palmer was five down against Thompson with seventeen to play, and lost by one shot. Gary Player was seven down against Lema with seventeen to play.

Gary Player did his homework and knew that he could win on the short holes when his lack of height was not such a handicap in driving. The short holes are the 2nd, 5th, 10th and 14th.

It was warm, the course well prepared and the two men went along with par for the first three holes and then Player got an eagle at the par five 4th.

They turned with Player one up – 34 to Lema's 35. They were soon on level terms just when Player could have expected to take a two stroke lead. It is a short hole with a shelf-like green. Player's second shot was five feet from the pin while

Lema's second shot ended in the grass and his third landed some twenty feet short. Lema sank his from 20 feet, Player missed his from five. Player was still only one up.

That lead went with the very next hole when Player drove off into the trees. Lema got up in two while Player just managed to get back onto the fairway. They were all square at the end of the 11th.

The twelfth has a line of trees across the fairway. Lema birdied the 12th, and the 13th, and the uphill 14th and the long 15th with its ditch, and the awkward 16th and the 571-yard 17th, regarded as one of the hardest par 5's in Britain. He won the dramatic 18th as well. Tony Lema came down the Burma Road in 29.

And Player? He was 6 behind with a 15 foot putt at the 18th. He holed it. Gary and Vivienne Player took lunch with Gary six behind and Lema looking better and better all the time. Lema relaxed at lunch. Player wolfed his down and tore out to the practice tee. He wanted to get rid of a hook in his swing, usually so smooth. By the end of lunch the ball was travelling true again. Or so he thought.

Lema teed off sweetly. Player hooked into the rough, lost the hole and was seven down. Seven down with seventeen to play. Player has never lost easily.

Player took two at the second, Lema a par three. The third is along a valley wooded with sombre rhododendrons and pocketed with fairway bunkers before the two-tiered green. Player birdied again and Lema got a par four. Five down with fifteen to play.

The 4th is a relaxed par 5, and they both got par. Five down with fourteen to play.

The 5th is a 167-yard par three. Both golfers were on the green in one, Lema 30 feet away, Player 15. Lema putted and the ball ran true. It lipped the rim of the hole and spun away. Player sank his and gave the air an uppercut. Four down with thirteen to play.

The sixth is an undistinguised par 4, and Player had a simple putt from two feet to get his par. Two feet. Two long feet, as Gary missed it. Five down and twelve to play.

'As we walked across to the seventh tee,' says Player, 'I

162

had an amazing spiritual experience. I've had them before, four or five times. I had it before the US Open, in fact before all four championships of the Grand Slam – the certainty that I was going to win. I'm not ashamed to say it was a message from God. It gave me a huge moral and physical boost, calmed me and yet charged me up to fight back harder than I have ever done before.'

Player and Lema shared the next three holes. Five down and nine to play, but only by the skin of Player's teeth for he sank a 15-footer at the nasty ninth.

'I kept thinking of my dad and my family and my country.'

Lema blundered at the short tenth, slicing down a bank and dropping a shot. Four down and eight to play.

Then they were back at the eleventh where Player had lost his lead before lunch. This time there was no straying into the woods; this time he drove close to the pin and holed the putt while Lema made par. Three down and seven to play. After the 12th it was three down and six to play as they halved.

Player, confident after his big drive at the 11th, sent the ball soaring down the fairway. Lema hooked into the bush. From the bush he managed to scuffle back onto the fairway. Player drove to within ten feet of the hole. Lema got onto the green, 25 feet from the hole. Lema putted first, and holed it. Lots of people have missed 10-foot putts even when there is no pressure, but Player sank his. Two down and five to play.

The crowd grew, the buzz increased, Lema's confidence started to wobble, and 'I was thinking more positively,' said Gary Player.

14 and 15 were halved. Two down and three to play.

The 16th is a par 4, not difficult, not particularly long but there are trees to the left which can block the approach to the green. Player took a driver and launched into the ball, attacking for all he was worth. His position was perfect. Lema took a 3-wood and hooked into the trees. One down and two to play.

Back they came to the ugly Par 5 17th with its dogleg to the left. Go too far to the right and you are in trouble. After two shots Player was 15 feet from the green, Lema over 80 feet. Lema pitched to within nine feet of the pin. Player chipped closer – by about a foot. Lema putted first – and sank it. Pressure was on Player now. He sank the putt, and the huge gallery roared. One down and one to play.

The 18th is also a par 5 with a dogleg to the right.

Player and Lema both put their drives on the fairway, Player closer to the green. Lema's second was short of the green. Player took a 4-wood and threw every ounce of muscle and energy into his second shot. 'I thought it was an awful shot.', he said. It must have been the best awful shot Player ever played. The crowd at the green told him that as they shouted their welcome to the ball as it rolled up the green. On the way it flew through the treetops, pitched and broke left, squeezed past the right-hand trap and took the curve of the ground nicely until it finished 10ft from the hole. The result was magnificent, but the ball had taken a line some eight feet to the right of the one he had hoped for.

Player's birdie left the game all square and a sudden-death play-off to come. Player had lost eight such play-offs in the USA but nobody would have bet on Lema at Wentworth that day, not after Player's second round charge.

In fact it took only one hole to finish the game, the hole where Player had hooked into the rough just after lunch to go seven down.

Player took two shots to the green on this stiff, par 4 hole. Lema's second dropped into the bunker. His shot out of the bunker ran 15 feet beyond the hole. Lema's putt ran and just slipped past. Player had two shots in hand to win the hole. Now he was not reckless and attacking. He pushed up close and then he dropped the putt. Gary Player had won the semi-final of the Piccadilly World Matchplay at Wentworth. And there was none of the Player ebullience in victory; he slumped to the ground, head in hands.

The next day Player showed no nervous reaction in beating Peter Thompson 3 and 2 in the final. There are people who believe that Player played better golf in winning that final. There are others who believe that he was even better – and Player would agree with them – when he beat Jack Nicklaus in the 1966 Piccadilly final. He won it again in 1968, 1971 and 1973. But then there can have been fewer golfers as competitive as Gary Player and matchplay is highly competitive.

Tony Lema? He accepted defeat graciously. From a poor family he had graduated from caddy to assistant professional, to head professional and then on to the tough American circuit. He battled for five unsuccessful years on the circuit till things came right in 1962 when he was 28. In August 1966 he and his wife were tragically killed in a plane crash on their way back from a golf tournament.

TRENT BRIDGE

Contrast, as the great poet Gerard Manley Hopkins observed, emphasises. It's true for colours, it's true for shapes, it's true for music, it's true for mood. Nothing worsens the depression of defeat than the expectation of victory and nothing heightens the exhilaration of victory like the expectation of defeat. Contrast is also an ingredient in humour.

"An Englishman doesn't know much about champagne," Tiger Lance, the finest allround sportsman I have known, said to me when he got back from the 1965 cricket tour to England. And he had visual evidence for his declaration.

First he showed me a newspaper headline: SPRINGBOKS POUR CHAMPAGNE ON PITCH. He also had a photograph, an amateur photograph in black and white, much thumbed, showing some Springboks, ridding themselves of urinary excess on the pitch which had in fact not deserved such treatment as it had been most kind to them. But they were an excited and triumphant band of young men that evening at Trent Bridge cricket ground in the English city of Nottingham. They had done what no other South African side had done for thirty years – won a rubber in England, and they had done it with such style, elan, panache as befitted the best team in the world, and the best team South Africa had ever produced.

After the exhilaration of Trevor Goddard's young team which performed miracles in Australia, came anticlimax of the dullest series of them all when Mike Smith's English tourists won the first test on a lunatic wicket in Durban and then ground out four consecutive draws. Geoff Boycott thought Mike Smith "a superb captain". He was not liked in South Africa. So much expected, and then the long yawn.

166

When the Springbok team set off for England, little was expected. After all Cheetham's side had lost there in 1955 and McGlew's in 1960. Now Trevor Goddard and Johnny Waite had retired, Joe Partridge was left out, and Tony Pithey withdrew after being selected. History was against the Springboks. Twelve South African teams had already visited England, nine had played tests and only one had won the series – back in 1935. In fact South Africa had won only five of 41 tests played in England.

Peter van der Merwe was the new captain, not a great cricketer and a relatively unproved leader, a dignified and intelligent man.

The Springboks start to the tour was ghastly. They came after the New Zealanders when the English season was well on its way and for the first time ever lost to Derbyshire who in turn lost their fast bowler, Harold Rhodes, for throwing. There were seven matches before the first test and the Springboks won only one – over Minor Counties.

England, left to get 191 in just under four hours to win the Lord's test ended with a streaky 145/7 and a draw.

There were two remarkable happenings on the Springbok side. Peter Pollock knocked out John Edrich with a bouncer. The second was Colin Bland, arguably the greatest outfielder the world of cricket has ever seen.

Barrington was England's top scorer in the first innings and played the ball towards mid-on. He ran. Colin Bland was at midwicket. He dashed, stooped and let fly. Barrington was yards out. When Bland let fly his aim was a single stump. Bland also ran out Jim Parks in the same innings. As Peter Pollock said of him, "His mere presence on the field, patrolling the covers like a hungry lion, saved us runs, for batsmen refused to take the slightest risk."

Up to Nottingham they went, full of confidence. The Pollocks were especially confident. After all Graeme had got a double century and Peter 7/51 against Kent. The Trent Bridge test was a triumph for South Africa and the two who made it possible above all others were the brothers Pollock.

Let Graeme tell the story; starting with the team talk at the Black Boy Hotel on 4th August, 1965:

These are a regular and important feature of South African Test match preperations. The whole team gets together under the captain's chairmanship; the strengths and weaknesses of all the opposing batsmen are discussed at length until a plan evolves how best to attack each one. And just in case the main plan should fail, we also plot alternatives.

Everyone has his say, then Peter van der Merwe finally decides what is to be done, ensuring that we all understand his strategy in detail, whether closely concerned with it or not. It is better for everyone to know exactly what is happening at all times. Some of the field placings decided upon are very complicated, but before the meeting ends we know them all inside out.

This time we decided that since the uninhibited Barber liked to play all his shots off the front foot we would keep deliveries to him short of a length to try and force him back. As far as he was concerned we reckoned it would be largely a case of "skittle alley" tactics.

We knew Boycott to be a good, stubborn player with a broad bat, but we thought we had a chance of trapping him into a false stroke outside his off-stump, the dodge he'd fallen for at Lord's.

It was difficult to pinpoint faults in Cowdrey's technique. If he were in the mood he would be a danger. Equally dangerous was Ken Barrington, but since Ken favours on-side play we voted to attack him outside the off-stump, also to test him early on with the odd bouncer.

It was no secret that Mike Smith was always vulnerable to pace at the start of an innings, and we reckoned to give him a hot time of it.

Our tour committee decided to make one change from the Lord's team, introducing left-armer Athol McKinnon in place of off-spinner Bromfield. We were uncertain at the time of the final composition of England's pace attack. In the event we were to find ourselves facing the 6 ft. 7 in. giant David Larter, lively John Snow of Sussex, and Tom Cartwright, the Warwicks-

Karen Muir and Ann Fairlie had many fine tussles. Here Karen emerges victorious once again

Sea Cottage (nearest camera) just gets up to dead-heat with Jollify in the July Handicap of 1967

Ray Mordt scores the try that put the Springboks level at 22-all in the Eden Park thriller in 1981. Frank Shelford, Dave Loveridge and Alan Hewson are too late to stop him

Zola Budd breaks the world record for the 5000 m at Stellenbosch in 1984 (photo: Anne Laing)

hire medium pacer who moves the ball off the seam and would obviously be able to take advantage of overcast weather conditions. But since we now had most of our batsmen in good trim, we felt equal to the best attack England could muster.

So, having already won the game "on paper" the night before it was due to start, the team repaired to the local cinema for relaxation, and to enjoy one of its favourite Westerns "The Magnificent Seven."

The Trent Bridge Test was the turning point of our England tour. It was also the setting for an innings I played in which everything I attempted came off. Yet things didn't go just as we planned, not by any means.

We were delighted when Peter van der Merwe won the toss. Whereas the Lord's wicket had been quick at first, then slow when rain fell on the second day, this one looked pretty true and reasonably fast. As the weather forecast was uncertain, it looked a good toss to win.

We all thought the sun that shone twenty-four hours before the match would have removed most of the moisture from the pitch. We should have known better. All our thoughts and schemes went haywire and agonisingly wrong at the start.

Eddie Barlow and Tiger Lance struggled against John Snow and David Larter, but it was the medium pace of Tom Cartwright which really caught us with our pants down. He wobbled the ball about, and occasionally one deviated off the wicket. Lance and Lindsay went for a measly 16 runs. When I came in, Eddie was still unusually tentative. At 42 he, too, departed; caught low down by Cowdrey in the slips, off Cartwright.

Cartwright was still swinging the ball in the air and off the wicket. But even at this stage, with two men out and England crowding us, I was not unduly worried. Then Colin Bland went one run later and things did begin to look black. I wasn't sure whether Colin was run out or stumped until later.

He lunged forward and trapped the ball with the

bottom of his bat and Jim Parks whipped off the bails before Colin knew what was happening. It turned out that he was stumped.

I suppose I ought to have been thinking of playing defensively for a while at least, but I just can't play that way. The only form of defence that I know is to attack. So when Ali Bacher came in I was determined not to let Cartwright and Titmus get right on top. I have always been rather partial to bowlers of Cartwright's type and I went after him. At lunch we were 76 for 4.

If I may say so without appearing too brash, the situation still did not worry me. I knew that I was in good form and seeing the ball well. In fact, this was one of those days when I felt comfortable from the first ball I received. Ali had appeared to have dug himself in quite nicely when he dragged a ball from Snow on to his wicket just after lunch. That made us 80 for 5 and I saw Peter van der Merwe glance at the huge and detailed Trent Bridge scoreboard as he made his way in.

I knew what was in his mind. It looked as if we were going to be bundled out for around 150 and then England would have the use of the wicket after it had dried right out. The skipper said nothing to me, but it was obvious that he was going to get his head down and hope I could continue to chase the bowling.

Peter Pollock remembers:

I couldn't bear the tension. I locked myself in a backroom as Peter van der Merwe joined Graeme at the crease. Graeme was looking good and he was taking the fight to the Englishmen. Whatever the cost he was going to the aggressor, working on the theory that attack was the best form of defence.

With the help of Van der Merwe, who merely kept his end up, Graeme took the England attack, particularly Cartwright, in his teeth and shook it like a dog does a rag doll. Before his innings ended, Graeme was being compared with legends like Stan McCabe and Frank Woolley. Personally, and I am sure all the other Springboks agreed, our Graeme Pollock on that day was beyond comparison with anyone.

His 125 was brutally brilliant and yet, you could never use the word brutal to describe such charm and elegance. Even the doyen of English cricket writers, Jim Swanton, was lost for words, such was the magnificence of Graeme Pollock. In the 70 minutes after lunch, Graeme and "Murphy" put on 102 runs.

When Graeme Pollock got to 28 he became the youngest batsman to score 1000 runs in test cricket. His innings lasted 162 minutes and included 21 fours. Graeme continues:

> I would be less than honest if I said that I did not enjoy the things that were said about me afterwards. After all, I was only twenty-one, and what kid of that age wouldn't be dazzled? The English Press were especially kind, and I must say that the applause from the Nottingham crowd was generous. My walk back to the dressing-room was unforgettable.

And when he came out he was upset. Tiger Lance tells me that Graeme threw the gat at his bag and said, "Gee, I was out of touch." He was also upset because he did not believe that he was out. Colin Cowdrey took a "catch" off Tom Cartwright, and Graeme was given out. He believes that he had hit the ground.

Peter van der Merwe made 38 and Richard Dumbrill 30 before South Africa were all out for 269, nothing like the score they had made in their team talk, but better by far than it promised to be at 80/5.

England had a half an hour to bat and Peter Pollock to face. It was a decisive period in the match.

Pollock bowled to Geoff Boycott, who got an edge. The ball flew to Tiger Lance at second slip. He juggled but held on. In his second over Pollock struck again when Barrington played on and England were 8/2. But Colin Cowdrey got his head down and, thanks to a dropped catch by Lance in the slips off Richard Dumbrill at 71, scored a century. England ended only 29 runs behind South Africa. Peter Pollock's figures were 5/53.

South Africa did not have opening batsmen when they went back to the crease. To start with Tiger Lance was not really an opener and then Eddie Barlow had a damaged toe and Denis Lindsay was sent in with Lance. At the close South Africa were 27/1, with Lance out. That had taken two days and, English weather permitting, the test looked headed for a result.

After being 35/2 when Lindsay went to Larter, South Africa's fortunes revived as Barlow, Ali Bacher, and Graeme Pollock got runs before the last six wickets fell for 96 runs and South Africa were 289 all out, a lead of 318.

Graeme takes up the story:

> We were fully aware that England had never made 300 in their fourth innings to win a Test match, but did not put too much reliance in precedent. Records are there to be broken. The wicket was still true, and England had the batsmen to do it.
>
> "It's going to be close, and this last forty-five minutes might be the crucial point of the entire series," the skipper told us between innings. We needed one wicket badly, and would be better pleased with two.
>
> In my brother's second over he had Barber caught at the wicket and the scent of victory was in the air. If England could have fended us off and started the fourth day with a clean sheet and bags of time at their disposal we would have been struggling.
>
> Then, in the last over of the day, McKinnon had Titmus caught and we saw John Snow emerge from the pavilion to face the last few balls. This meant that the England batting order had been disrupted, so Jim Parks would probably be coming in as late as number 9.
>
> It was a controversial move by the England captain. There are arguments for and against the employment

of a night watchman. My own view is that in a situation like this an established batsman should be sent in to take his chance. After all, a strokemaker like Parks could change the whole complexion of the match, but not if he were to be left with a couple of tail-enders – which was what the use of a night-watchman implied.

Smith had used two tailenders. Snow was soon gone on the morning of the fourth day and England were 10 for three. Jackie Botten bowled to Ken Barrington and Denis Lindsay could not hold the difficult chance. Then Barrington hooked at Pollock, and England were 13 for four as Cowdrey joined Boycott. The two batsmen dug in against the eager Springboks. Then Cowdrey went to glance burly Athol McKinnon, lifted a toe just a little and Denis Lindsay had the bails off, a decisive and brilliant stumping.

South Africa had not been doing well in the first innings when Graeme Pollock decided to attack the bowling. England's tactics were different, as Graeme Pollock observes:

> Joined by Peter Parfitt at 41 for 5, Geoff Boycott now went right back into his shell, persisting in uncompromising defence and making no attempt to score at all. He seemed to view the pitch with the gravest suspicion, but it was not the pitch which caused England to fall into such a perilous position.
>
> I know it is easy to be wise afterwards, but rigid defence is seldom the answer to a situation like England were in. I appreciate the need for some caution, but I ask you, could two and a half hours batting to produce 16 runs ever be justified?

McKinnon bowled dour Geoff Boycott, and then England attacked. First Peter Parfitt and Mike Smith went after the Springbok bowling till a remarkable bowling change brought a break-through. Peter van der Merwe tossed the ball to Graeme Pollock. With his third delivery, a top spinner, he had Mike Smith lbw, one of Graeme's four test wickets.

Then Parfitt and Parks really got after the bowling, and

there was an interruption of half an hour for rain, after which the ball was slippery and the batsmen went on their merry way. When they came together England had scored 12 runs in 270 minutes. The next hour produced 80 runs.

Peter Pollock is the man to take us through to well after stumps:

> I said we were worried. That would be an understatement. The damp conditions had taken the edge off our fielding and bowling. I was beginning to visualise the match slipping away for the first time in my cricketing life I secretly asked God to help our cause. I was fielding down a fine leg and I even suggested a "deal". If God allowed us to finish it off I wouldn't have a celebration drink that evening. I promised to abstain.
>
> Next over, I was summoned by Peter van der Merwe. Success didn't come straight away but then it did, a few overs later, it was most spectacular. First Parfitt played across the line and was clean bowled. I don't think I have ever been more relieved to see someone head back to the pavilion. In the same over Tom Cartwright went lbw and only Larter stood between South Africa and victory.
>
> There were a few close shaves but Larter decided on a policy of attack. He got away with a few streaky shots and then attempted just one too many. Trying to drive he lofted the ball towards mid-off. There, waiting under it was skipper, Peter van der Merwe, his big hands looking the size of the Grand Canyon, ready to swallow the small, red, ball.
>
> It was like an eternity waiting for it to drop out of the sky but finally it did and as Peter tossed the ball heavenwards, the whole team erupted in sheer joy and elation. Our frustrations were over. We had finally beaten England.
>
> I don't think that I have personally had a prouder moment in my life than when I was allowed to lead the team off the field, having taken a further five wickets in the second innings for a match tally of ten. In our

changing-room it was sheer chaos with all the well-wishers around and with the bubbly flowing.

But, personally I had made a "deal" with God and I was going to stick by it by not having any drinks.

What happened in the first three hours after victory was great fun. Some of the Springboks even ventured onto the pitch in their underpants and performed the famous "jukskei" march, with Field Marshall Athol McKinnon in charge. Even some of the local constabulary joined in – one to the extent that he was severely reprimanded the next morning. It was a night to remember and the celebrations continued into the small hours of the night.

As for my "deal". Well, I honoured it for about two hours, then I nipped off quietly into the shower room and suggested to the Lord that I had, in those two hours, said my thanks. I felt I got my answer in the form of one of the constabulary who had seen me take off and had followed me with a beer. He insisted that I have a drink and I took this as the "sign" that I could now go off and enjoy myself.

Trent Bridge – just the mention of this ground will still stir the emotions of any of the Springboks involved in the 1965 Springbok tour. It was an unbelievable experience.

WORLD RECORD AT 12

As Zola Budd is to athletics, so Karen Muir was to swimming - at the start of their careers at least. They came suddenly on the scene, gawky and shy, everybody's little sister. And they both broke world records.

There were controversies surrounding both though Karen Muir's little haggles about money, arguments about her coach, her father's appearance on an overseas tour, and the debates about her moving from Kimberley to Pretoria, are pale and insignificant beside the grand manner of the battles which have raged about bewildered and innocent Zola. Zola got to the Olympics and Karen didn't. Zola's Olympics was a sorrowfull affair, anyway. And in 1988 they stopped her going at all just as Karen Muir was excluded in 1968. But then, and only in Std. VIII and fifteen years of age, Karen Muir had proved over and over that she was the best in the world.

For some of us it was hard to acknowledge her greatness at first as we were loyal to the memory of Joan Harrison who had won a gold medal at the Helsinki Olympics in 1952, the only South African swimmer ever to win a gold medal.

Years later, it is probably safe to confess that I was hopelessly in love with Joan Harrison and was desolate when a photograph appeared in the paper of her on the back of some East Londoner's motor cycle. But really, the truth is that even without an Olympic medal Karen Muir actually did greater things in the swimming pool and captured the imagination of the nation in a way Joan Harrison did not do.

Few people would associate dry and dusty Kimberley with swimming, but in 1962 there was a great swimming coach in Kimberley, Frank Gray. Also living in Kimberley at the time were Dr. Ronnie Muir, a veterinarian, and his striking wife Yvonne, who enjoyed society life in the diamond city. Determined and confident Yvonne Muir could not understand the painful shyness of her nine-year-old daughter but the daughter who had learnt to swim the previous year enjoyed the water.

Nothing but the best for Yvonne Muir and off she went to Frank Gray, an Englishman who had settled in Kimberley a few years before, and asked him to coach the girl. "Karen doesn't believe she can do anything right," her mother told Gray. "Teach her to swim and perhaps that will take her more out of herself."

Frank Gray remembers that day in October, 1962. "She was a shy little girl of nine, with her head buried in her chest, standing just behind her mother. She never looked at me once while I spoke to her."

Gray started his coaching that very day. She could crawl, he noticed, but she preferred swimming on her back.

Gray did not believe in pushing a swimmer too hard but Mrs Muir was very determined, and as success started coming so her determination increased, as did Frank Gray's involvement till there were regular battles between mother and coach as each sought to direct the shy girl's energies, and many of the battles left Karen crying.

Karen had a coach, she worked hard, and she had courage. Gray said, "To reach the standard that Karen has at her age takes courage. There are no short cuts – only hard work and dedication to condition the body to the physiological and psychological stress."

While Karen was working her frail frame in Kimberley, there was in Johannesburg a young girl of thirteen with a deadly desire to win – Ann Fairlie. That year, 1963, she broke the South African 110 yards backstroke record and in 1964 she won both the 110 yards and the 220 yards backstroke.

In 1964 Frank Gray was coaching Vernon Slovin, the Springbok butterfly swimmer, who was off to the USA to take up a sports scholarship. "We gave Vernon a little farewell party – just my swimming squad – and I made a small speech wishing him luck. I said he was our best chance of a world record even if he got it in the United States. Karen, who had been with me for two years then, came to me

177

afterwards and shyly asked me what the world record for the women's backstroke was. I told her. Later her mother revealed to me that ever since that time Karen had nursed a secret ambition to break this world mark."

They took a small Springbok swimming team to Europe in 1965. Karen was taken along for the experience. She was then 12 years of age, in Std. V at Diamantveld Primary School. The real backstroke swimmer was Ann Fairlie, then 16 years of age, the South African backstroke title holder. South African hopes were pinned on her beating Linda Ludgrove, the British holder of the world record. Ludgrove was beaten and her record broken but not by the same person.

There was no hint of a miracle ahead when the Springbok team gathered in Johannesburg and trained in the short ($16\frac{2}{3}$ m) pool in Hillbrow. Other coaches around the world preferred longer pools; the South Africans felt the shorter ones developed explosiveness in the water. Mind you the South African coaches were largely imports – Gray from England, Bob Campbell from Australia, and Jan Kooiman from Holland.

There was no hint of what would happen when the Springboks swam in Barcelona, and Ann Fairlie won the 100 m backstroke in 68.2 seconds – the fourth fastest time ever for the distance. There was no hint of it either when the little group, managed by Alex Bulley, moved on to Holland.

The British championships that summer were in Blackpool. August is holiday time in Britain and Blackpool is *par excellence* the working man's holiday place with its tower, bingo halls, booths with bearded ladies and fortune tellers, zoo, piers with concert halls, dancehalls, punch and judy shows on the beach, seven miles of tiered promenade, donkey rides, and – for the brave – even some bathing. Blackpool has a population of less than 150 000 but each year more than seven million holiday makers visit the Lancashire town.

The British Championships were held in the huge indoor stadium. Ann Fairlie was pitted against Linda Ludgrove. Karen Muir was not entered for the senior backstroke – far too young for that. Instead she was entered for the Girls' Event. Up till then her best time for 110 yards backstroke was 72.2 seconds. The most that was expected of her was to reach the final of the girls' event.

Karen Yvette Muir was 12, stood 5 ft 1 ins, weighed 108lbs. It was the Japanese who had lowered the age for top swimmers at the Los Angeles Olympics in 1932 with their motto – The newer, the faster.

"Young swimmers," they said, "can be compared to an aeroplane with a large engine and light fuselage. The youngsters have large hearts and strong lungs in proportion to the rest of their body, and that is why one can expect teenagers to do well in international competition." In fact they measured this power-mass ratio in mililitres per kilogram as a result of measuring oxygen consumption at various rates of exercise.

Young is fine, twelve is ridiculous, not even teenage. This thin gawky girl with the long arms caused no flutter of interest when she slipped into the pool. Just over a minute later she was sensation, and the crowd roared fit to beat the bands down the Golden Mile. And all this happened in a heat of the Girls' Event.

Karen Muir pushed off powerfully and went straight into the lead. She reached the turn, 55 yards away, five yards ahead of the rest in a time of 32.4 seconds. Now everybody was watching the girl they were to call the torpedo – the Timid Torpedo but a torpedo.

As she reached the five-yard marker the crowd started cheering. The timekeepers went into a busy huddle, and a jubilant Alex Bulley grabbed Karen as she rose out of the pool and kissed her, as he had done to Joan Harrison in Helsinki thirteen years before, when Karen Muir was not yet born.

The announcement came: "Karen Muir of South Africa, a new world record -". That's as far as the announcer got as the crowd erupted. The Springboks, led by Ann Fairlie, rushed to their teammate, flashbulbs popped, reporters, taken by surprise and unprepared, shouted questions while the swimmer snuggled closer to her manager and the team's captain, Geoff Gryls, gave her a kiss. Laughing and cheering, the Springboks carried Karen to her dressingroom while the reporters and photographers jostled behind. A woman photographer even chased Karen into the showers to get a picture.

Back in the quiet of her hotel Karen Muir was able to watch herself on television, a medium still a decade away in South Africa.

What she had done was become the youngest competitor ever to hold a world record, the first South African to hold one for swimming. And it had all happened so quickly. Joan Harrison in the Fifties had been circumspect about it, going from stage to stage, starting at 12 as the Border champion, winning the Olympics at 15. Karen Muir seemed to leap straight up at the sun at the first attempt. It was certainly one of the most dramatic, unexpected moments in South African sport. Karen Muir had swum the 110 yards backstroke in 68.7, 0.8 seconds faster than Linda Ludgrove's record.

Alex Bulley claimed to have foreseen it. "Karen is a natural. When she did 70.6 seconds in Spain recently I knew she was capable of a record." But not, apparently, capable of swimming in the senior event. "When reporters asked me about her, I said Karen was going to provide a shock. And she has."

Ann Fairlie swam after Karen's feat and, almost unnoticed, beat the former holder of the world record and broke what had been the record by 0.6 seconds. The Fairlie-Muir clash would dominate backstroke swimming in South Africa for quite some time, but always Karen Muir would hold the limelight, even when Ann Fairlie beat her and took the world record off her in her own swimming pool in Kimberley in February, 1966, just six months later. Ann Fairlie's time was 68.6. Ann Fairlie became the first South African to break a world record for swimming in South Africa, and yet the focus was always on Karen Muir who seemed to get more publicity from the fact that *her* record was broken than Ann Fairlie did in breaking it.

Five days later Karen Muir powered back – at the national championships in Durban, an easier pool, with a time of 68.3.

There were other great backstroke swimmers about at the time – Kiki Caron of France, Cathy Ferguson of the USA, Suzuki Tanaka of Japan, and Elaine Tanner who was known

180

as Mighty Mouse. Karen, who grew rapidly from the scrawny girl who won in Blackpool to 5 ft 10 ins and 148 lbs, beat them all and broke world records on no fewer than 17 occasions.

She did not get to the Mexico Olympics, of course. No South African did. But she did get back to the British championin 1967, in Coventry this time, and again she beat Linda Ludgrove and broke a world record, this time Ann Fairlie's and by now the time was 67.5 seconds. The year after that she knocked a full second off that time.

In July 1966 she broke the world 200 m backstroke record in Beziers (France) and bettered it at Lincoln in the USA. In August that year she broke the 220 yards backstroke in Canada.

She said of her swimming, "Sometimes I feel good and then the records come." One was taking more than a second off her own world record for the 220 yards backstroke when she swam in Pretoria. At the halfway mark that January, 1967 she was only 1.9 seconds outside the world record for the 110 yards backstroke!

There is no doubt who the queen of women's backstroke swimmers was in the Sixties – Karen Muir of South Africa, breaker of 17 records, winner of numerous trophies and awards, including South Africa's Sportswoman of the Year and the Helms Foundation Award. Her formula for success: sheer love of swimming.

Nowadays Karen Muir is a doctor in Ladysmith in Northern Natal and she has no interest in swimming at all!

JULY MIRACLE

It all started in June, 1966. But what happened then is part of the miracle of the July Handicap 1967 – and all the drama, the stuff that legends are made of.

Nightclub bouncers are not normally early risers, as the nature of their job dictates. But Johnny Nel was up early two mornings in a row. The first time he found it exhilarating; the second time was a rude awakening.

In South Africa hunting is largely a winter sport – biltong time. Riding out into the veld to hunt is as old as the existence of guns in South Africa. What Johnny Nel did was to cause such revulsion and anger that a pseudonym was frequently used to protect him even when he was in gaol. You see, he shot a horse.

Sea Cottage was not just any horse. He was the darling of the nation. Never has a horse in South Africa captured the imagination the way Sea Cottage did; never has a horse in South Africa featured in the press the way Sea Cottage did. He was the Karen Muir, Zola Budd, Naas Botha, Graeme Pollock, Morné du Plessis, Viccie Toweel of horse racing all rolled into one and without any nastiness. Everybody loved Sea Cottage – everybody except Johnny Nel and a bookmaker, that is.

Syd Laird says, "I love all my horses, but there will never be another Sea Cottage. That horse and I were great mates." And Syd Laird had been there from the beginning.

Syd Laird had an uncle, Syd Garrett, who trained a brave mare called Maritime, which was sent to Sid Birch for breeding purposes. Syd Laird persuaded Sid Birch to pair Maritime with Fairthorn. Unseen, Syd Laird persuaded the Birch Brothers to lease him the result of the union.

Laird charged down to Dordrecht to see the foal whose near fore turned out very badly. "I could see then why they'd agreed to lease me the horse. I got him to the stables as quickly as possible and got the farrier to start gradually paring the hoof away. In no time he was perfect." The foal was, of course Sea Cottage.

Sea Cottage, with Bobbie Sivewright up, easily won its first race. "We got the best price we ever had on him," says Laird. When Sivewright was involved in a car smash, Bert Abercrombie rode Sea Cottage in his second race, the Festival Juvenile Handicap at Kenilworth. It would be the only time when Sea Cottage's jockey was not Bobbie Sivewright, Syd Laird's brother-in-law. But Sea Cottage won. He won his first five races.

By June 1966 Sea Cottage , now a three-year-old, after another six wins, was 6 to 4 favourite for the July. Bookmakers stood to lose a fortune. One decided not to take a chance. His weapon – Johnny Nel, armed with a short-barrelled German pistol, loaded with a soft-nosed (lead) 6.75 mm bullet.

A string of horses belonging to Syd Laird was passing under the bridge over the Umgeni River north of Durban's city centre. They were on their way to Blue Lagoon Beach. It was 6.10 on the morning of 10th June, 1966. Johnny Nel was lying in wait up on the bridge. "Nobody from the beach could see the car and shooting from there, nobody could see me. It was a perfect vantage point."

Lean Sea Cottage with his white blaze, attended by two grooms, one riding with the other behind, was easy to recognise. In the concrete shelter at the south end of the Rupert Ellis Brown Viaduct, Johnny Nel, nightclub bouncer, squeezed the trigger.

"I had no intension of killing the horse. Cripple a leg and he doesn't run. Simple as that. As soon as I was certain which of the horses was Sea Cottage, I aimed at the rump and fired. I was firing down at the horse about 30 or 40 feet away.

"I saw the horse bolt and that was enough. I knew I had hit him. I jumped into the car and put my foot down hard.

"I felt alive, exhilarated – like a man at war."

Laird had been suspicious enough or careful enough to put another horse with a blaze at the front of his string, normally

Sea Cottage's position, but Johnny Nel was not fooled. He hit the right horse.

Sea Cottage shuddered and reared, but the groom got control. Had it been a car backfiring? Then they saw the trickle of blood from Sea Cottage's right upper quarters.

"I was staying at the Athlone Garden Hotel," says Syd Laird, "which is not far from the Blue Lagoon Beach. When I got to the Beach that morning Cookie Amos's brother, Boet, ran over to me and said, "Your horse has been shot!" I laughed and told him that was the only thing that would stop Sea Cottage from winning the July.

When the truth finally dawned on me I was panic stricken. I jumped back into my car and sped off for the stables. I caught up with Sea Cottage alongside the Windsor Park Mashie golf course. I jumped out of my car and saw where he had been shot. I walked right back to the stables with him, by which time he was in shock and bleeding from the quarters. I was totally dazed. I couldn't believe that anybody could do that to my horse."

On the way back to Newmarket stables Sea Cottage kicked out wildly and then – horror – lameness set in. When the vet reached the stables, the horse was sweating and shivering, but still warm from the walk. Then he would not put the leg to the ground. The vet said, "There was tremendous bruising. We did not probe the wound, but treated him for shock, pain and bruising. We made three attempts to locate the bullet by X-ray but without result. We did not probe the wound because we assume the bullet is sterile because of the great speed at which it travels.

"We knew that no bone or major blood vessel had been damaged and that no nerve had been severed.

"Sea Cottage was a magnificent patient, as gentle as a kitten and a gentleman to work with. He made an unbelievably fast recovery, because he was such a fit horse."

The July was three weeks away and the vet didn't give him "a chance in hell of running."

Molly Reinhardt recalls. "As the news spread round the country, newspaper offices and radio switchboards were jammed with telephone calls from thousands of indignant and enraged well-wishers. Telegrams arrived at the New-market stables by the hundreds, letters poured in from young and old, from racegoers and from hundreds who had never set foot on a racecourse. Many of the letters and "Get Well" cards were addressed to the horse himself. Typical was a postcard which read: "Sea Cottage I wish you all the luck for the July. You are a very nice sweet horse and I love you very much." Mrs. Elvia Rayner, a former SABC piano soloist, wrote a piece of music about the horse, and Des and Dawn Lindberg wrote a ballad. Bookmakers offered R2 000 reward for information which would led to an arrest.

Johnny Nel was awake early the next morning as well. Three policemen from Durban's Murder and Robbery Squad knocked on his door at three in the morning and arrested him. Three days later he appeared in court on a charge of "malicious injury to property".

Meanwhile Syd Laird said to himself, "I'm going to beat those swine." And six days after the shooting Sea Cottage did a slow canter, flinching with each stride but keeping going.

There were two more arrests, but eventually only Johnny Nel, who was paid R100 for shooting a horse worth R75 000, went to gaol – to Sonderwater for six years, three of which were suspended. Before they took him away, Nel said, "Of all the strange missions, good or bad, in my life, the one thing I'm not proud of is the shooting of Sea Cottage. It doesn't take much intelligence or guts to shoot a horse."

Obviously the exhilaration did not last. A gaol sentence tends to reduce the fun, and so does becoming the most unpopular man in the land.

The bookmaker who had engaged Nel, did not go to gaol but he was kicked out of Tattersalls and ceased to have rights as a bookmaker.

Miracle number one – Sea Cottage ran in the July. Miracle number two – he started 2 to 1 favourite. There is not quite a fairytale ending as he did not win. Bobbie Sivewright felt he could have won but, "as we approached the two-furlong mark a horse went into Cuff Link who in turn was forced onto Sea Cottage. Syd Laird trained the winner, Java Head, while Ajax and Fire Eyes were second and third. *The Sunday*

Tribune's headline the next morning ran: "Java Head great, but Sea Cottage was magnificent."

Miracle number three – two weeks later Sea Cottage won the Clairwood Winter Handicap. It's no wonder that the horse which won 20 of his 24 races became a legend.

No July Handicap, however, can compare with the July of 1967, when the bookmakers really suffered.

Let Molly Reinhardt, wife of Fred Rickaby, the trainer of Jollify, describe it:

> Unquestionably the greatest thriller of them all was the fantastic dead heat in the Durban July Handicap of Sea Cottage and Jollify, in 1967.
>
> Never in the long glittering history of the July have there been such scenes on the Greyville course.
>
> The crowd went mad as the two horses crossed the line in the most sensational finish in the history of the race. Crowd hysteria almost took over as the judges puzzled over the photo-finish photograph and then called for a second one. There were emotion-packed scenes as punters steamed to the winning enclosure screaming "Sea Cottage". Others yelled "Jollify". The tension mounted when Jockey Sivewright went into number two box and John Gorton rode Jollify into the winner's enclosure.
>
> Mrs. Sydney Laird was sobbing, Mr. Laird had tears streaming down his face, Mr. Fred Rickaby, the trainer of Jollify, was dazed and speechless and Mr. Chris Saunders – joint owner of Jollify with his father, Mr. Douglas Saunders – kept on saying: "Wait for the result . . . wait for the result." Mrs. Chris Saunders was lint-white and kept on saying: "It's a dead heat. It's a dead heat."
>
> At first Jollify's supporters went wild, until the rumour got out that Sea Cottage had won. Fred Rickaby, told that Jollify had run second, said: "Oh, well, we gave them a ruddy good go". Syd Laird, overcome with emotion, leapt on to Sea Cottage's back to the hysterical roars of the crowd. But the big drama was still to come with the official announcement of a dead

heat. Pandemonium was displayed, the glass box was smashed when excited punters stormed forward to see the amazing picture.

Mr. Rickaby said to a newspaperman: "Everyone is pleased to see the first and second favourites finish as they did. I am proud to think that Jollify could even it out with such a great horse as Sea Cottage". Everyone was pleased – except the bookmakers, who reported taking the biggest beating in years through the dead heat of the first and second favourites. Both horses were bred by Birch brothers.

When the owners, Mr. Saunders and Mr. Laird, led their horses on to the track for the victory canter down past the stands, a unique problem cropped up. There was only one blue riband, for nobody in their wildest dreams had visualised a dead heat in the July. The sash of victory was shared and held by jockeys John Gorton and Bobby Sivewright between them before the cheering crowds.

The cold facts of this sensational race are best retold in the word of the winning jockeys. Bobby Sivewright told the reporters crowding round him in the weighing room: "Sea Cottage jumped very well and was lying third or fourth until the eighth-furlong post. Then he dropped back. Nearing the straight I eased Sea Cottage up a bit and sighted Jollify slipping through on the inside. Coming into the straight Sea Cottage began to move up and at the false rail was in about 4th position. I had a clear run down the middle of the course but towards the finish Sea Cottage tired slightly and started shifting in towards the inside fence. I fought out head by head with Jollify over the last half-furlong."

This was the second big race in which Sivewright rode a dead heat. He rode Response when she dead-heated with Tiger Fish in the 1958 Clairwood Winter Handicap.

When John Gorton rode confidently into the winner's enclosure, Fred Rickaby asked him: "Did you win?" Gorton rolled his head back in a sigh of relief and said: "Yes". Later when questioned about his confidence Gorton said that about a hundred yards before the post he was in front and he could see Sea Cottage coming at him from behind. He said: "I was in front then. I put my head down and rode and rode. I rode right past the post, and when I looked up, I was still in front so I naturally thought I had won. Sea Cottage must have caught us right on the post and then faded. I was half-a-length in front when I looked up, about 20 yards past the post."

Bobbie Sivewright also had this to say, "I was carried out wide that day, otherwise I would have won comfortably. However, to this day I still think that I won that race. I am adamant I passed Jollify in that last stride."

Sea Cottage at 11-10 started the shortest priced July winner on record. Later, a strong magnifying glass was placed over the photo of the finish and not a fraction between the noses of the horses could be detected. Mr. Harry Oppenheimer, whose horse King Willow came third, said: "This is the greatest race I have seen".

Young Gorton, then 21, carrying 2lb overweight, rode a brilliant race, which Syd Laird described as "a superb piece of riding," and which Jollify's trainer Fred Rickaby called "faultless". His ride was a brave as well as a splendid one, for two weeks before he had had a miraculous escape from a dangerous fall. He had hurt his foot so badly that there was at that stage strong doubts about his chances of being able to ride.

He received daily treatment by a specialist who at one time was dubious that he would be able to ride in the July. However, padded stirrups and a boot which had to be cut eased the pain he felt before the race. A few months after winning the July John Gorton was sent to England on a visit as a "thank you" present by owner Chris Saunders. He was introduced to the racing world of Newmarket by trainer Fred Rickaby and made an immediate impression.

Sir Jack Jarvis offered him the plum job of first

jockey to his stable and John left South Africa for England where he has been riding with considerable success. In the 1972 season he finished among the top 10 jockeys and is stable jockey for Bruce Hobbs, who has over 100 horses in training.

Triumphing over a gunman's bullet and carrying 127lb to Jollify's 100, Sea Cottage broke then the South African record for stake earnings with a total of R92 537.

A fitting postscript to the most dramatic finish of any July was the presentation made by the Durban Turf Club to Mr. Jack Bradford, the club's official handicapper. Mr. Bradford was given a gold watch suitably inscribed to commemorate his feat of bringing off a handicapper's dream – a dead heat in a major handicap.

Both horses went to stud – Jollify in the USA, Sea Cottage after winning his last race, the Cutty Sark Stakes at Germiston, back to Dordrecht where it had all started. There the grooms called Sea Cottage's off spring The Children of the Bullet.

Sea Cottage died in March, 1987, and was buried under a tree on the farm after they extracted from his body a bullet which was given to Syd and Marlene Laird.

Was he the greatest horse ever? Bobby Sivewright rode both Colorado King and Sea Cottage whom he called Joe. "Colorado King was a better horse than Sea Cottage," said Sivewright.

That may be so, but no horse in South Africa's history captured the imagination and affection of the nation the way Sea Cottage did, and no race has had the drama of the 1967 Durban July.

THE LORD MAYOR'S SHOW

Picking great moments from the two home series against the Australians, the last official cricket tests played by South Africa, is difficult in the extreme, not because they are so few, but because they are so numerous.

Denis Lindsay bludgeoned the Australians and still holds the batting record for a wicket-keeper in a test series: 606 runs for an average of 87.57 in 1966-7. In one test he scored 182 runs and took six catches, the most dismissals by a South African wicket-keeper in an innings in a test.

There was the bowling of Peter Pollock and Mike Procter in the first test at Newlands in 1970, Trevor Goddard's bowling in the first test at the Wanderers in 1966, Graeme Pollock and Peter van der Merwe at Newlands in 1967, the Pollock brothers batting together, Tiger Lance's six for glory in Port Elizabeth in 1967 to sum up South Africa's superiority over Bobby Simpson's Australians, Ali Bacher and Tiger Lance in partnership for Transvaal in 1966, and so many more.

We have taken one moment, because it may just have been the finest day's batting in the history of test cricket.

In the summer of 1966-7 South Africa won a test against Australia in South Africa for the first time and celebrated by winning the series 3-1 with one drawn. Bill Lawry brought the Australians back for more in 1969-70 when Ali Bacher took over the captaincy from Peter van der Merwe and the gulf between the two sides was enormous. It was men versus boys, athletes versus the handicapped. It was certainly the highlight in South Africa's cricket history. And for once the Springboks were not apologetic. They knew they were far better and went for it.

The Australians, in their run-up to their visit to South Africa, had no premonition of disaster. They had beaten

England, the West Indies, and India, while the Springboks were slumbering without cricket. It was a giant which slept, ready to leap awake refreshed.

There were new men in the Springbok side – Barry Richards and Lee Irvine amongst them. And the first test was at Newlands where South Africa had not won for 60 years. But history did not matter.

Barlow got a century and South Africa made, with more plod than panache, 382. Australia went into bat that Friday afternoon as the crowd swelled in anticipation of the week-end. Soon they were roaring in a fashion more suited to the rugby ground across the railway line.

Keith Stackpole opened with Bill Lawry who had revealed an insatiable lust for runs in the run-up to the test. On the stroke of three Procter started his long run to bowl to Stackpole. Peter Pollock had second use of the ball into the wind from the Kelvin Grove end. In his second over with the score on 5 he struck.

Bill Lawry walked inside the second ball of Pollock's second over and was bowled without offering a shot as the ball cut back from outside the leg stump. Ian Chappell, the best batsman in the world, according to Bill Lawry, got a rising ball off the last ball of that same over and hooked. Lee Irvine leapt upwards and his outstretched hands deflected the ball upwards and Graham Chevalier made the catch. Now the crowd was roaring.

After tea, with the score at 38/2, Procter struck. Stackpole got an edge and Eddie Barlow made no mistake, trotting away gleefully with the ball. Then Ian Redpath got an edge and Barlow dived to take the catch inches from the ground. Graham Chevalier got a wicket and so did Kelly Seymour, and Australia were 108/6 at close. A hoarse crowd left the ground.

The Springboks did not force the follow-on, but batted dourly again and won the test by 170 runs. The bowling was fine but the batting gave no inkling of what was in store for the Australians, mystery spinner Gleeson and all, when they got to Durban, where Lance and Traicos came in for Seymour and Chevalier.

Ali Bacher won the toss, and Goddard and Richards came out to bat. I suppose it could be considered arrogance, but Richards set out quite deliberately to try to score a century before lunch, and his skipper who came in when Goddard went for 17 with the score on 88, went along with him till he was run out trying to give Richards the strike in the over before lunch. Richards had to be content with 94 not out at lunch.

After lunch Graeme Pollock joined the rampant Richards. It was a moment to dream about, but let Peter Pollock, who was there, describe it:

An hour after lunch, twelfthman Ashley Mallett was ready at the player's entrance with the drinks and while he waited he watched Richards being clean bowled by Eric Freeman's slower ball. But what had happened in that 60 minutes, the Oxford Dictionary and all its superlatives could not do justice to. In that hour, Graeme Pollock and Barry Richards added an unbelievable 103 runs.

Never had South African test cricket enjoyed such utter domination. In simple terms, the formula was pretty basic. Pollock took the one crease, Richards the other and between them they peppered the pickets with an array of shots that were majestic in execution and brutal effectiveness. I just couldn't believe my eyes and when Barry was eventually out, the poor shell-shocked Aussies stood at the wicket applauding Barry all the whole way back to the pavilion. Lawry waited until the Springbok had left the field before summoning the drinks, which was a fine gesture.

Next man in, Eddie Barlow, lasted a very short while but when he got back to the pavilion he remarked "It was like after the Lord Mayor's show. There is no room for me out there. Those two have made a mockery of batting". And indeed they had.

What a pity that there had not been any television cameras around to record those soaring sixty minutes. The rest of the innings belonged to Pollock and he

192

proceeded, in the same classic vein, to chalk up one record after the other.

Ironically enough, this was Graeme Pollock's first century at Kingsmead, which had been a "hoodoo" ground for him over ten years of first-class cricket.

At 210, he reached his personal highest first-class score; at 233 he beat Dudley Nourse's record against Australia and an on-drive off Keith Stackpole which took him to 258 saw him past Jackie McGlew's all-time record of 255 for a Springbok batsman in tests. It seemed that he was just not going to stop and that for once and all he was going to allay his late father's fear that he couldn't really pile them on when a lazy, weary forward defence prod, not quite to the pitch of the ball, presented Keith Stackpole with a simple return catch. Graeme's 274 had been out of a total of 558 and he had also shared in a century partnership with Tiger Lance. The Springboks finally finished at 622 for nine wickets when Ali Bacher, mercifully, decide to declare.

The second day of the second test had its memories, stirring if not as exhilarating as the partnership between Richards and Pollock, but then what could ever hope to be?

The Australians were going along quite happily and had reached 44 without loss when Barlow was given the ball. Ten balls later he had taken 3 for 4! Trevor Goddard also got a wicket and when the umpires closed play for bad light the Australians were 48/4. They struggled manfully but the test ended, a day early, with victory to South Africa by an innings and 129 runs, the first time South Africa had ever defeated Australia by an innings.

At the Wanderers they won again, this time by 307 runs and down in Port Elizabeth they completed the grand slam of victories over Australia with victory by 323 runs. Barlow and Richards got second centuries in the series and Lee Irvine managed to get his first while Bacher and Lindsay got a few. Procter, Pollock, and Barlow took most of the wickets.

Then the curtain came down on test cricket for South Africa, but what a grand (if sad) finale! And nothing would beat the majesty and power of Pollock and Richards at Kingsmead on 5th February, 1970.

THE SCOREBOARD

Second Test, played at Kingsmead, Durban on February 5, 6, 7 and 9

South Africa won the toss

SOUTH AFRICA
first innings

B. Richards b Freeman	140
T. Goddard c Lawry, b Gleeson	17
A. Bacher b Connolly	9
G. Pollock c and b Stackpole	274
E. Barlow lbw b Freeman	1
L. Irvine b Gleeson	13
H. Lance st Taber, b Gleeson	61
M. Procter c Connolly, b Stackpole	32
D. Gamsy lbw b Connolly	7
P. Pollock not out	36
J. Traicos not out	5
Extras (b 1, lb 3, nb 23)	27
Total (for 9 wkts dec)	622

Falls: 1-88, 2-126, 3-299, 4-231- 5-281, 6-481, 7-558, 8-575, 9-580.

Bowling: G. McKenzie 25.5-3-92-0,
A. Connolly 33-7-104-2
E. Freeman 28-4-120-2
J. Gleeson 51-9-160-3
D. Walters 9-0-44-0
K. Stackpole 21-2-75-2

first innings

K. Stackpole c Gamsy, b Goddard	27
W. Lawry lbw b Barlow	15
I. Chappell c Gamsy, b Barlow	0
D. Walters c Traicos, b Barlow	4
I. Redpath c Richards, b Procter	4
P. Sheahan, c Traicos, b Goddard	62
E. Freeman, c Traicos, b P. Pollock	5
B. Taber c and b P. Pollock	6
G. McKenzie c Traicos, b Procter	1
J. Gleeson not out	4
A. Connolly c Bacher, b Traicos	14
Extras (lb5, nb 10)	15
Total	157

Falls: 1-44, 2-44, 3-44, 4-48, 5-56, 6-79, 7-100, 8-114, 9-139.
Bowling: M. Procter 11-2-39-2
P. Pollock 10-3-31-2
T. Goddard 7-4-10-2
E. Barlow 10-3-24-3
J. Traicos 8.2-3-27-1
H. Lance 2-0-11-0

second innings

K. Stackpole lbw b Traicos	71
W. Lawry c Gamsy, b Goddard	14
I. Chappell c Gamsy, b P. Pollock	14
D. Walters c G. Pollock, b Traicos	74
I. Redpath not out	74
P. Sheahan, c Barlow,b Procter	4
E. Freeman, b Barlow	18
B. Taber c Lance, b Barlow	0
G. McKenzie lbw b Barlow	4
J. Gleeson c Gamsy, b Procter	24
A. Connolly lbw b Procter	0
Extras (b 9, lb 8, nb 22)	39
Total	336

Falls: 1-65, 2-83, 3-151, 4-208, 5-222, 6-264, 7-264, 8-268,
        9-336.
Bowling: P. Pollock 22-5-45-1
          M. Procter 18.5-5-62-3
          E. Barlow 31-10-63-3
          J. Traicos 30-8-70-2
          T. Goddard 17-7-30-1
          B. Richards 3-1-8-0
          H. Lance 7-4-11-0
          G. Pollock 3-1-8-0

South Africa won by an innings and 129 runs.
Umpires: G Draper (Natal) and C. Coetzee (Eastern Province).

A BIZARRE OCCASION

"We all knew how important this game was going to be, probably the most important game we'd ever play!"

Andy Dalton, captain of the All Blacks was the speaker, and the match he was talking about was the third and final test between the Springboks and the All Blacks at Eden Park, Auckland, in 1981. How final that test would turn out to be one cannot yet tell, but it certainly had an air of finality about it as an aeroplane flew overhead bombing the players with flour bombs and a horde of demonstrators protested the presence of South Africa's rugby players on New Zealand's playing field.

It was a test match to grip the throat and leave it dry, a test match to numb the mind, to stop the heart and freeze the blood. It was the saddest of all endings, and yet a match of momentous importance.

The Springboks were again, after a decade's absence, on the fields of traditional rivals. It seemed to say that it would be possible for traditional rivals to visit South Africa again. And yet, somehow one knew, this was the end. No game was worth splitting people in two or causing so much upheaval.

And on the field, too, there was that day, 12th September, 1981, the saddest of possible endings. It was a sad moment and yet one of the most memorable. There are still today people in South Africa who do not like Nelson Mandela but who would be far happier seeing him walking down a Pretoria street than Clive Norling, referee of that third test who made two decisions deep in injury time which cost South Africa a deserved share of that bizarre match.

The whole tour was bizarre and yet in the midst of all the stress and the strain there was so much to admire in the spirit of rugby football and above all in the intensity of matches between South Africa and New Zealand. As Andy Dalton said afterwards, 'Matches against the Springboks are the pinnacle for the All Blacks. If those two teams don't compete in future, it just won't be the same.' And Andy Dalton's father was the vice-captain of the All Black team which toured South Africa in 1949, the whitewashed All Blacks.

The Springboks had not been to New Zealand since 1965, the year when the Prime Minister of South Africa, HF Verwoerd, at Loskop Dam announced to the world that Maoris would not be allowed to tour South Africa with the All Blacks and his faithful bleated their approval. Two years later his successor, BJ Vorster, told the MCC that Basil D'Oliviera was not allowed to tour South Africa because he was 'coloured'.

Three years after that the Maoris came with the All Blacks, and it would not be long before the South African government would be helping cricket to pay huge sums of money to bring out all manner of black cricketers. So much for the prophetic vision of two Prime Ministers. But the damage that they had done would live and grow long after their deaths. It was into the eye of the storm which these two men had brewed, that the 1981 Springboks would ride.

New Zealand was in a turmoil. The nation was split and families were split on the issue, but because they valued individual freedom they allowed the tour to proceed and the forces of law and order tried to tiptoe between protecting those who wanted to play against the Springboks and allowing other citizens the opportunity to protest against those whom they saw as the emissaries of apartheid. Whatever the wisdom of allowing the tour to go ahead and however unseemly much of the action during the tour was, the government of New Zealand did state clearly its belief in its citizens' freedom of choice, association and speech – a freedom they were more prepared to suffer for than most nations.

It was a dangerous and violent situation. People were arrested, policemen and others were hurt, the Waikato match was stopped by invasion and the South Canterbury match was cancelled to give the police a chance to rest. The Springboks learnt to live with bomb scares, police protection, sleeping in unusual surroundings before matches – such as squash courts and rugby changerooms – dressing in mufti, waiting for hours under stands for matches to start, and then playing to hostile noises, protected by police and barbed wire.

And yet when they got together four years later, the Springboks unanimously voted that they would tour again even in those dire circumstances, because they had had so much fun, amongst themselves and with the generous folk of New Zealand, and because playing the All Blacks is the zenith of any Springbok's rugby ambition.

In fact the quality of the rugby in the three tests is testimony to the calibre of the players who took part and their rare dedication which enabled them to concentrate even with a mad bomber overhead.

The first test went New Zealnd's way more comprehensively than the 14-9 score suggests. But the Springbok forwards smashed back and the second test was won 24-12, the highest score the Springboks had scored against the All Blacks ever.

And so to Auckland, and all to play for . . .

A touring team always has a special identity – an island of home in a hostile sea. The desire to do well builds up. In their special circumstances the Springboks desire to do well was enhanced. There were supporters from home, hoping. And the captain was confident.

The man destined, so it seemed, to lead the Springboks in New Zealand was charismatic Morné du Plessis. His premature retirement shocked the nation. Wynand Claassen took his place though it seemed that the tour management did not like the idea. Theuns Stofberg was the captain for the first test but Wynand Claassen was back for the victorious second. And he was there for the third – to lead a patchwork side as De Villiers Visser and Stofberg withdrew through injury, Hennie Bekker went on with an injury, Willie du Plessis and Gysie Pienaar were replaced during the match, apart from other injury problems.

Forget the bomber, forget the fighting in the streets outside Eden Park, forget the slogan-shouters, forget everything extraneous. Concentrate just on the match as the players did – with a total absorption which is a miracle of rugby football, perhaps the loudest testimony to the desire the players of the two countries have to compete against each other – and to win the competition. The fact is that it was a great match.

The greatness of the players' skill and nerve made the anticlimax of the end, the pathetic bathos of it all, chillingly mortifying. And the man who orchestrated the end was Clive Norling, rugby refereeing's bandmaster. It was an ending unworthy of such a match, of such players.

The Springboks who were playing, spent the night in the comfort of the Eden Park Hotel – under the Grand Stand of the great ground. To be fair it was comfortable. New Zealanders, more than anybody else, know how to get rugby things right. And, any way, have you ever met a nasty New Zealander? It was comfortable but it was also a long, long wait. You get tired and numb. You yawn, you stretch, and your mouth goes dry. How could you possibly play with such lassitude? Then its time to change, for Augie Cohen, surely the most attentive and popular doctor a rugby team could ever have, to attend to areas of stress, time for urgent words, for muttered encouragement.

The curtain-raiser – between the Under 21 teams of Auckland and Counties – ended in victory for Counties, and already the plane was flying overhead, dropping bombs. Then it is out onto the field with its cricket pitch, and it's time for Clive Norling, tall, black-haired, upright with red jersey and socks, which announce that he is Welsh, and tiny shorts. The arm is up, the whistle goes, and the game is on.

For the Springboks it looked all over very quickly. After Allan Hewson and Naas Botha shared a penalty apiece, the New Zealanders surged ahead into what seemed an unassailable lead.

Stu Wilson scored a fine try when Allan Hewson cut through, committed Gysie Pienaar and sent the right wing over. Then Doug Rollerson – he and Naas did not find each other mutually attractive during the series – kicked a penalty and the All Blacks were 10-3 up. And still it was all New Zealand as Clive Norling took less interest in their line-out activities than he had done in Christchurch.

From a scrum Mexted drove for the line and fell short. He did something funny on the ground and the ball came back.

Big Frank Shelford went to pick up the ball and knocked it on. It wasn't a big knock but a knock doesn't have to be big for a scrum to be awarded to the other team. There was no scrum. Instead Gary Knight picked up and heaved himself through Divan Serfontein's arms over for a try which Rollerson converted to give the All Blacks a 16-3 lead.

Let there be no moans about the try. Referees have all got themselves into awkward positions. They have all missed things. It happens to every one of them in every match he referees. It's not worth debate, – just recording. In fact there were no complaints in the Springbok camp about it. Nobody felt 'robbed'.

The half-time score was 16-3 to the All Blacks. That is a substantial lead, and it was a fair reflection of All Black domination. In the third test at Lancaster Park on the 1965 Springbok tour of New Zealand the Springboks had been down 16-5 at half time and won the match 19-16.

In tests between the two countries the All Blacks have only once turned a half-time deficit into victory and that was in the very first of all tests – in 1921 at Athletic Park when the Springboks led 5-0 and finally lost 13-5. On the other hand the Springboks have six times been behind at half-time and eventually won the match. But 16-3 on this of all tours? A tall order indeed.

Like New Zealand rugby, South African rugby has pride, and in the second half they also had the wind, on that mean Auckland afternoon while the plane kept on sometimes lower than the height of the Grand Stand. At one stage the announcer asked the spectators not to throw missiles from the ground at the plane in the air!

Play started for the long second half. The longest in test rugby? It would not stop till fifty one and a half minutes had elapsed. There will never be a half with as much drama. There will never be a match with a sadder ending.

Just after the restart smoke bombs were thrown onto the field, and a minute and a half later play resumed. (The time lost for stoppages in this half is material.)

Seven minutes later Colin Beck, substituting for Willie du Plessis, chipped, and Ray Mordt raced past Hewson to score.

Naas Botha converted and the score was 16-9.

New Zealand made her first sortie into South African territory after a quarter of an hour in the second half as Andy Haden charged. Johan Heunis, on for Gysie Pienaar, stopped him with a solid tackle. New Zealand won the ball and South Africa was penalised for off-side. 19-9. That's a steep hill, even with the wind.

It did not take long for South Africa to get back into the picture. Ray Mordt, hemmed in on the right-hand touchline, kicked a lobbed ball ahead and powered after it. It bounced, and he snatched it from in front of Hewson and Steve Pokere to score. Botha converted. 19-15.

There is an incident which I should like to describe. I don't think anybody else has written about it because it seems trivial but in the argument surrounding the game it is not.

There was a scrum after 21 mins 50 secs, All Black ball. Dave Loveridge bent to put the ball in. Robert Cockrell, the South African hooker, struck for the ball. In doing so he definitely lowered his body. Then Loveridge put the ball in. It was heeled by New Zealand but Murray Mexted at number eight immediately knocked on. Scrum, South Africa ball.

Cockrell had infringed twice before that. The scrummage law of the time stated: 'While a scrummage is forming and is taking place, all players in each front row must adopt a normal stance. Both feet must be on the ground, must not be crossed and must be in a position for an effective forward shove.' It also said: 'No front row player may raise or advance a foot until that ball has touched the ground.' Robert Cockrell was doubly wrong but he was not penalised though clearly New Zealand got no real advantage from the scrum.

Forget about the lowering business because Andy Dalton did it frequently with impunity, which means that on that score there was consistency if not accuracy. But Cockrell was penalised later in the match for lifting his foot early in circumstances more dubious than the one related and where he got off scot free. Players like a referee to be consistent, at least in the same match.

South Africa attacked down the left when Gerrie Germishuys picked up a stray pass. Murray Mexted killed the ball and was penalised. That also was harsh as it was the sort of day when the ball was regularly massacred. Botha goaled. 19-18 after 22 minutes – and no stoppage other than the minute and a half at the beginning of the half.

Now there was a long stoppage for injury to Loveridge. It lasted a minute and twenty-two seconds. Total stoppage time so far – 2 minutes 52 seconds. Add another 15 seconds to remove a fallen missile – 3 minutes 3 seconds. Then there was another smoke bomb and another 32 seconds' hold-up – 3 minutes 35 seconds.

Doug Rollerson got into trouble, and as he moved away from it, Divan Serfontein nearly decapitated him. Clive Norling got hold of Wynand Claassen and Divan Serfontein and gave them a long lecture. During this lecture Gary Knight was hit by a flour bomb. He was ready to resume when Norling ended his lecture on the evils of headhunting. Take that as a stoppage and you now have 4 mins 39 secs, sermon and flour bomb included. When Norling went across to see to Knight, he asked the first aiders to go easy with the water or 'you'll have him covered in pastry'!

Danie Gerber was caught as the Springboks tried to run in front of their goal posts. The All Blacks won the ball and Rollerson lobbed over a dropped goal. 22-18 after thirty nine and a half minutes. There was half a minute to play plus stoppage time.

The Springboks attacked and after 42½ minutes in the second half there was a stoppage for injury to Loveridge near the All Black line. The injury lasted half a minute. Stoppage time now 5 mins 9 secs.

Then the Springboks struck. Colin Beck was tackled but shovelled the ball out towards Ray Mordt. As it bounced Naas Botha kicked it through, gathered the bounce, swerved infield and took three men out of the game as he fed Ray Mordt. Mordt powered through Loveridge and scored as Frank Shelford tried to smother him. There was a long stoppage now as Loveridge was hurt in the tackle. It lasted 1 min 35 secs. Total stoppage time now: 6 mins 44 secs. Naas Botha had to wait all that time to take the conversion and missed. 22-22.

After all the time taken for Loveridge's injury Mexted found himself with an 'injury' somewhere down his leg. The stoppage of 29 secs gave Mark Donaldson time to come on to replace Loveridge. No sense playing with 14 men when you can have 15, is there? Stoppage time: 7 minutes 13 secs. But when Mexted's injury started, the half had already run 46 minutes 50 seconds, six seconds more than the maximum stoppage time in the half.

After 49 minutes in the half (or a minute and 47 seconds beyond the time when the final whistle should have gone) Norling awarded a scrum when the ball became dead. It was slightly surprising that he awarded only a scrum to the Springboks as right in front of him Andy Haden twice punched at Flippie van der Merwe's face. Perhaps he did not connect or perhaps Flippie's reaction was too bland to warrant a penalty. But the award of a scrum makes what happens next even more bizarre even within the context of this bizarre match.

The scrum was another mess as the All Blacks went down earlier than the Springboks and had to be moved back. Then the scrum went down while Divan Serfontein waited with the ball tucked under his arm. He started to bend, but the scrum wheeled towards him. Only one Springbok scrum in the whole of this long match had not wheeled towards Serfontein and everytime he had stopped and pushed on the scrum, appealing to the referee, and everytime he had been allowed to get the scrum straight. This time there was a whistle and a free kick was awarded to New Zealand. Serfontein turned to face the referee in bewilderment. Serfontein says 'I did not know what was going on. During the whole game I had told him that I couldn't get the ball in but he did not do a thing about it. In the second test he had blown them often for the same thing.'

Apparently poor Robert Cockrell had lifted his foot. Clive Norling says he did. In the May 1985 edition of *SA Rugby* Cockrell says, 'I did not flash. But I moved my feet. I had to move my feet because the scrum was wheeling suddenly. But I did not strike for the ball.'

On the otherhand Andy Dalton believes that Cockrell was

'foot-up'. When Serfontein turned to see what the referee was up to, Donaldson grabbed the ball from under his arm, put it on the ground, tapped it, and ran – towards his left and slightly forward before passing to Rollerson whom the *forwards* tackled some 12 metres from the original mark. The law here is important. In 1981 it stated: 'The opposing team must retire without delay to or behind a line parallel to the goal lines and ten metres from the mark or to their own goal line if nearer to the mark ... Retiring players will not be penalised if their failure to retire ten metres is due to the rapidity with which the kick has been taken, but they must not stop retiring and enter the game until an opponent carrying the ball has run five metres.'

Clive Norling, says Donaldson ran 'some two metres'. If Donaldson did not run five metres, he has the smallest strides in international rugby. And the five metres run need not be forward. Certainly, too, the kick was taken rapidly. But none of that meant a thing. Penalty. And Allan Hewson goaled it and punched the air. The half had now run 51½ minutes. And it would dribble on just a little more before Norling released the tired players.

When Loveridge was injured for the first time – before Mordt's try and after 2½ minutes of injury time and with the score at 22-18 in favour of the All Blacks – Wynand Claassen the Springbok captain, asked the referee how much time was left. Wynand Claassen in his autobiography says, 'He replied that it was to be the last scrum.' Rob Louw in his autobiography says, 'I heard Wynand talking to Clive Norling who seemed to say that this was the last scrum of the match. I wasn't 100% sure, so I asked Mr Norling how much time we had left. He said clearly, "This is the last scrum of the match."' From that scrum the Springboks scored to level the scores. The last scrum of the match occurred 6½ minutes after that 'last scrum of the match'. What a telling scrum it was.

I remember getting back into bed after watching the television broadcast of the match and struggling for breath and trying to swallow from a dry mouth, – and I still get a horrible feeling. Imagine what the players felt like as they trooped bewildered from the field.

It was a momentous match. It will always be tough for South Africans to say that the All Blacks won that particular test or that the Springboks lost it. The only fact is that the All Blacks ended with more points after Clive Norling got in on the act. The record of the match in *Centenary – 100 Years of All Black Rugby* states, 'The tourists were desperately unlucky not to share the series.'

When all is said and done, remember what Boy Louw always said, 'Looks at the scoreboard.' The scoreboard will be the same 'to the crack of doom' – New Zealand 25 South Africa 22 in the final test at Eden Park on 12th September, 1981.

PURE GOLD

There he stood, arms straight up in the air in triumph while 75 000 people roared. It was one of those moments to savour, full of meditative material for years to come, but above all a moment of glory. The man who stood there in the north east corner of Ellis Park wore a Springbok jersey, and he was black. Somehow he expressed the triumph of more than just one man.

In the twelfth minute of the second half of the second test, Richard Hill, the England scrum half, punted the ball a few metres downfield and into touch some six metres outside his team's 22, on South Africa's left.

Chris Rogers, whose throwing in had not always been accurate, threw to number 4 in the line-out, and up rose Schalk Burger to take it with both hands. He played it quickly down to Okkie Oosthuizen sweeping round from the front of the line-out. He turned and flicked the ball back to Divan Serfontein who sent it flowing to Errol Tobias at fly half. Tobias moved somewhat across the field with John Villet outside him. Suddenly there was Danie Gerber cutting back from the outside centre. From now on everything happened at top speed as the English spread in defence.

Gerber took the switch pass, evaded a man and was speeding down the left hand touch line with Carel du Plessis gliding up on his outside. Gerber gave to du Plessis as the Springboks swept forward. At full speed du Plessis, hemmed in on the touch line, dropped the ball low onto his left foot and chipped in-field. John Scott, the England captain and lock, was back for the ball and took it in the air, but Gerrie Sonnekus, the Springbok number 8 who had played scrum half for the Springboks a decade before, drove into Scott's back and the ball popped loose.

207

Up to gather the bouncing ball was Hempies du Toit, the powerful tight-head prop. He turned and, arms partly held, fed back to his fly half, Errol Tobias going right. Tobias turned to shield the ball and, arms grasped, dropped it in the direction of Avril Williams, the wing so strong on his feet. Still the English defence reformed and put pressure on the attackers, and Williams cut back towards the haven of his forwards who rallied to him.

Rob Louw went in and brought the ball out going left. Then came a moment of genius as Louw stopped and played the ball back towards the right touch-line and gently into the hands of Divan Serfontein. The scrum half immediately fed Johan Heunis, the fullback but now in the fly half position. Under pressure Heunis got a great pass out to his left to John Villet who straightened and fed Tobias who had managed to get back to form a backline and was now in the position of an outside centre as the Springboks improvised. Williams got back outside Tobias who was just outside the English 22 and about 10 metres in from touch. Despite the speed of happening the English defence was in a good position and it was a two-against-two situation – Tobias and Williams against John Palmer and Mark Bailey.

Tobias hesitated slightly, produced a tiny dummy, and, as Palmer checked, he went for the outside gap. Palmer, who had hurt his nose moments before in tackling Johan Heunis, flung himself at the fly half. A decisive hand-off saw the Englishman sprawl to the ground as Tobias accelerated for the goal line 22 metres away.

He straightened for the line, running smoothly, head tucked into neck. As he went the crowd on the east stand rose in a wave with him, cheering and throwing their arms about. Mark Bailey stuck closely to Avril Williams who stopped to show his opponent what really was happening.

Huw Davies and Dusty Hare covered without much conviction as Tobias sprinted for the line, ending with a dive-like fall. A group of policemen in the corner cheered, and René Hourquet, the school principal from Orange in France, signalled the try.

Straightaway Tobias was on his feet. He stood tall facing

his team-mates and then flung his arms aloft in triumph. Smiling gleefully he rushed back to his side, hands out-streched to Rob Louw who came scuttling across in a rare display of Springbok elation. Hempies du Toit came over to put his arm around his fly half's neck and rub his head.

South Africa had stretched its lead to 29-3 in the second test of the series at Ellis Park on 9th June, 1984. The action could be seen in replay on the huge screen on the north side, just above where the live action had happened.

The Argentinians called Ellis Park the "cathedral of rugby". If that is the case, then Errol Tobias, the 34-year-old builder from Caledon, was a great high priest, as he stood arms aloft proclaiming all sorts of messages to the faithful.

One message he proclaimed was that his was no 'cosmetic' selection, but then only a madman would not pick the best available fly half. If you were indulging in cosmetics, there would be plenty of other places to hide an inadequate player.

He also proclaimed that even without Naas Botha, who was trying to sell his talents to Dallas Cowboys, South Africa could win test matches convincingly. In fact in two tests with Tobias as fly half South Africa scored nine tries. Running rugby was winning rugby and it was fun. In the first half of that test Danie Gerber scored a hat-trick of tries. That was fun.

Errol Tobias played four times against England on their seven-match tour, and I have never seen a fly half play with such skilled aggression. In the slow motion replay of the try, Hugh Bladen, a former Transvaal fly-half, said, 'Not often you get an outside half with such incredible power.'

It was a great moment in the first test match played in the splendour of the new Ellis Park, the best appointed rugby ground in the world. And I was there.

As Errol stood there in triumph while the crowd cheered, one longed for the ability of a dramatic poet or the ex-pression of a bold artist to capture the various emotions of the moment, its colours, sound, and movement. Dick Greenwood, the English coach, summed it up by saying, "Errol Tobias is not coloured – he's pure gold."

ZOLA!

She was small, waif-like, vulnerable, timid – everybody's baby sister. Everybody? Not quite, because she was also white and a South African, and in the end she was to suffer to the point of breakdown, hounded out of Britain, the land of hope and glory. For so long she was in the headlines it is incredile to think that in 1987 she turned only 21.

Zola Budd had genius, starting at those bare feet on the end of long, spindly legs, and a fierce competitiveness behind that timid exterior. And yet she has been the starkest tragedy of the whole apartheid-induced disease that has infected South Afican sportsmen since 1967, a year after Zola's birth and the year when the Prime Minister B.J. Vorster told the MCC that they could not come to South Africa with Basil D'Oliviera in their team.

The little girl from the Orange Free State, to be dubbed by the press the hunted fawn, started running seriously in 1980 and was only 15 when she won her first women's titles for the 1 500 m and the 3 000 m, barefoot and all.

When she was sixteen she set world junior record times for the 1 000 m (2:37,9) 5 000 m (15:35,67), and 3 000 m (8:46,41). Then came 5th January, 1984 at Coetzenburg.

She came down from Bloemfontein with her coach, Pieter Labuschagne, a 38 kg child who rose at 6.30 each morning to run 10 km to be followed by 10-12 km again in the afternoon. She had matriculated from Sentraal High School in Bloemfontein in 1983 with distinctions in history, biology, and business economics – a serious student like that earlier child wonder Karen Muir.

She had long legs, light bones, and a small body. She ate what she liked and loved pets. An innocent. Who could be nasty to her? Already people overseas were calling her the greatest woman athlete over middle distances the world had ever seen – Mary Decker, Maricica Puica and the rest notwithstanding.

The meeting at Stellenbosch was packed, and what a night it was! There was a fire under the grandstand, Johan Fourie just missed a South African record for the 5 000 m, Bethuel Seribe surged ahead to pip Matthews Temane at the post in the 3 000 m, Marius Hugo-Schlechter came from behind to beat Hans van der Veen in the junior 3 000 m, and there were other highlights and points of excitement. But nothing compared with Zola's race. After all, already a star, people would flock to watch her run. They would ask for 'two tickets for Zola, please'. Never in the history of South African athletics has one athlete so captured the imagination and in her time the only sportsman to compare with her high profile has been Naas Botha, but the images are different.

The seventeen-year-old girl (She turned 18 on 26th May, 1984), took off her Hoërskool Sentraal tracksuit and went quietly onto the track. Everybody was watching her. They were tense; 15 minutes or so later they would be hysterical.

Zola led from start to finish. She was in fact running a race against the clock and nobody else mattered. To break the world record, held by Mary Decker, she would have to average 72,5 seconds per lap. Her first lap was 69 seconds, the next two 70 seconds each. Then she slowed – 72 seconds, 71 seconds, 73 seconds, 74 seconds, two laps of 72 seconds.

Half way through the race she had lapped the whole field! Still she showed no signs of fatigue, no strain on her pert face. The crowd were on their feet, clapping and cheering, and even after she had finished she kept running, doing two laps of honour while they cheered and cheered and wept and cheered. They loved her, they were proud of her. She was the first South African to break a world record since Gert Potgieter in Bloemfontein in 1960. Her time – 15 minutes, 1,83 seconds, a record by 6,45 seconds, by a 17-year-old, delicate, South African girl, in Stellenbosch.

The first shadow fell the next day, and the nation stood angered. The International Amateur Athletic Federation would not recognise Zola Budd's record because she was a South African, and the IAAF did not recognise South Africa. You could be any other nationality and run a faster time than Mary Decker had done, and the IAAF would happily tell you that you were the world record holder. Let Zola Budd do it and they would not bat an eyelid. Mary Decker remained the holder of the world record.

Two months later Zola went to Britain, sponsored by *The Daily Mail* and a month later she was a British citizen, causing the wrath of those who had been longer in the queue. Before that she had been offered a marriage of convenience to be able to become British.

In her first race in Britain, at Dartford, she broke the junior 3 000 m record and she would go on to break six British and Commonwealth records, win the European Cup over 5 000 m at Crystal Palace, twice win the world cross-country title, and run in places like Belfast, Helsinki, Stuttgart, Lisbon, Moscow, and Los Angeles.

With all the political hooha which never left Zola who could forget the horror of that race with Mary Decker at the 1984 Olympic Games in Los Angeles, the pictures over and over of Mary Decker's stumble and fall, the anguish on Decker's face, the horror of the booing of 85 000 spectators in Los Angeles – 85 000 booing that little, timid girl? It is history that the inquiry cleared Zola of blame and fixed blame on Mary Decker. And in her rage Decker said, "I blame her." And she had many other things to say which were unkind.

Zola would not be out of all sorts of trouble from then on – loneliness, money squabbles, family upheaval, injury, and, apparently, bad advice from her last mentor, Fanie van Zijl, and finally, suspension by the IAAF who held a hearing at the Park Lane Hotel. Again the little girl seemed bullied. Again the nation wanted to put its arms around her. Again she came home.

At the time, Alan Robinson of *The Argus* wrote from London. We publish it in full as a salute to its brilliance of style and content:

> Zola Budd's international athletics career is probably over, but the immense psychological damage

that has been done to this introverted waif will never be repaired.

Her escape to the sanctuary of her family in South Africa was inevitable. Almost certainly she left Heathrow Airport on a single ticket to the oblivion she so desperately needs and seeks.

That flight home may well mark the final chapter in wretched story of human greed and political gutter-fighting in which a raw, tremulous and virtually unilingual 17-year-old was dumped in a foreign land to run for fame and fortune.

She achieved both in four amazing years, but is now paying the terrible price. Success on the track, some of it breathtaking and spectacular, was matched by ceaseless abuse, most of it nauseating and cheap.

Whatever else her succession of advisers and manipulators, coaches and cursers, friends and enemies had in mind for her, they certainly succeeded on two fronts:

- They created a world champion.
- They wrecked a human being.

Few people emerge with honour from this tragic saga of exploitation and evil intent. Perhaps it is expecting too much to hope that some will feel a twinge of conscience when they read the words of doctors who were, quite genuinely, horrified at her mental state.

In the words of Dr Ken Kingsbury, a sports medicine expert and official medical officer to many British teams: "She is a pitiful sight. Bouts of crying and deep depression.

"My assessment was that she was at the end of her rope. A dire state. Sweating, sleepless, suffering from headaches. I would have hated to see my daughter in such a condition.

That, it must be said, was the end product of individuals who spat at her in the name of freedom and democratic governments who rejected her like last week's rotten eggs.

There are people prominent in sport today who are equally guilty. They cringed in the face of threats and cowered at the very mention of boycotts. That human wreck who stepped off an SAA Boeing at Jan Smuts yesterday was the result of their handiwork, too.

I shall never forget the eminently forgettable look on the face of militant campaigner Pat Cheyney when he heard that the International Amateur Athletics Federation had effectively ended her career in a London hotel three weeks ago.

With the same lip-smacking smile of a hyena coming across the freshly abondoned carcass of a zebra, he uttered the immortal words: "That's finished with Budd. We've nailed her."

I hope Mr. Cheyney reads the words of Dr Kingsbury. I also hope he does not have a daughter.

Not all the central characters in this awful business are villains. Pieter Labuschagne was a coach of immense-ability and a genuine father figure in the early days.

Jannie Momberg and Graham Boonzaier rescued Zola from the post-Los Angeles Olympic scrapheap and I accept their interest was sincere. But their passports were South African and thus their motives were always suspect.

British mentor Les Jones was a shield and an inspiration, while coach John Bryant's involvement was both straight and committed.

There are those who claim this complex Free Stater was a strong-willed, determined and witting tool of the South African Government and its backers. That she had been sent into the outside world as a sporting ambassador for apartheid and oppression. That she was at the spearhead of the escape from the strange-hold of isolation.

They, clearly, do not know Zola Budd. Or they do not wish to.

I first saw and talked to her in Oslo in June, 1984. She was a pathetic sight, desperately clutching on to Labuschangne's arm. Hiding from the public, hiding from the minders sent by the *Daily Mail* to prevent media rivals from getting at their "exclusive" property.

And hiding, always hiding, from the scowling, chanting demonstrators.

She wore the frantic look of a hunted fawn. She had no fingernails left from the incessant chewing. And all she wanted to do was to buy her father a pair of slippers and her mother a scarf.

That was only the start. Later she was to be spat at during a race at Crystal Palace, bundled into a thorn bush during a cross-country event on Merseyside, booed by thousands of one-eyed Americans who watched her collide with Mary Decker in Los Angeles. . .

Her mother and father's marriage was to break up under the strain and injury took a year out of her career at its very peak.

Undoubtedly, there were people in South Africa who used her for their own purposes. She was wrongly advised and was led like a blindfolded sheep to places where she should not have gone.

Misguided patriots who forgot that there were ears and eyes beyond Randfontein and Brakpan said things that were to dog her from Gateshead to Auckland.

Yesterday's flowery speeches became today's lifeblood of the protest industry. Ill-considered Press statements in South Africa became damning quotes in the demonstrator's pamphlets. Although Zola stupidly spent far too much time away from her adopted country, the ordinary people of Britain were generous with their support and lavish with their praise. But ordinary people do not write the wounding words or train the close-up television cameras or scream obscenities at the side of the track.

In the end, the reed had to break. I fear it may never be mended. Broken bones may knit together again, broken spirits do not.

A wretched story indeed . . .

It would be only a wretched story if we were to forget that she was also the greatest of athletes. It would be only a wretched story were we to forget that magic night at Stellenbosch – a magic night in a magic town with that little girl who could make dreams come true.

BIBLIOGRAPHY

Springbok Saga by *Chris Greyvenstein* (Don Nelson)
The Fighters by *Chris Greyvenstein* (Don Nelson)
20 Great Springboks by *Chris Greyvenstein* (Don Nelson)
Giants of South African Cricket (Don Nelson)
For the Love of Rugby by *Rob Louw* with *John Cameron – Dow* (Hans Strydom)
More than just Rugby by *Wynand Claassen* with Dan Retief (Hans Strydom)
Centenary 100 Years of All Black Rugby by *R H Chester & N A C McMillan* (Moa)
Barbed Wire Boks by *Don Cameron* (Rugby Press)
Laws of the Game of Rugby Football (Various years) ·
Articles in *S A Rugby*, 1984-5
For the Record The Allan Hewson Story by *Ian Gault* (Rugby Press)
Boots 'n All! by *Andy Haden* (Rugby Press)
Pride of the Lions by *Reg Sweet* (Howard Timmins)
The Red Squad Story by *Ross Meurant* (Don Nelson)
Springboks in Wales by *John Billot* (Ron Jones)
100 Years of Rugby. The Story of the Villager Football Club. by *Dick Stent*
The M C C in South Africa by *P F Warner* (J C Juta)
The World of Cricket edited by *E W Swanton* (Michael Joseph)
The History of South African Cricket by *M W Luckin* (Horton)
Articles in *S A Cricketer*
Articles in *S A Sportsman*
Articles in *S A Sports Illustrated*
Articles in *The Cape Times, The Cape Argus, The Argus,* and *The Star*
The Protea Cricket Annuals
Rugby Writers' Annuals
South Africa in International Cricket 1888 – 1970 by *Brian Bassano* (Chamelon)
The Thirty Tests by *Peter Pollock* (Don Nelson)
The Allied Book of S A Sport and Sports Records
Southern Africa in Sport
Springboks 1891 - 1970 by *A C Parker* (Cassel)
Ruffled Roosters by *A C Parker* (Howard Timmins)
The Varsity Spirit by *Louis Babrow* & *Dick Stent* (Johnston & Neville)
A Short Cut to Rugby by *C K Friedlander* and *Patrick Tebbutt* (CNA)
Lions among the Springboks by *J B G Thomas* (Stanley Paul)
W P Rugby by *A C Parker*
The Fourth Springboks by *R K Stent* (Longmans)
The Guiness Book of Rugby Facts & Figures by *Terry Godwin & Chris Rhys* (Guiness) Wisden
Danie Craven by *Bun Booyens* (S A R B)
Craven by *Hennie Gerber* (Tafelberg)

The Springbok Story by *D H Craven* (Beerman)
Springbok & Silver Fern by *Reg Sweet* (Howard Timmins)
Springbok Glory by *Louis Duffus* (Longmans)
Out of the Magic Box by *Bruce Heilbuth* (Galvin & Sales)
Totsiens to Test Rugby by *Hennie Muller* (Howard Timmins)
The July Handicap by *Molly Reinhardt* (Don Nelson)
My Greatest Match edited by *Arthur Goldman* (C N A)
Long Innings by *Sir Pelham Warner* (Harrap)
Cricket in the Blood by *Dudley Nourse* (Hodder)
Springboks Down the Years by *Danie Craven* (Howard Timmins)
Bouncers and Boundaries by *Peter & Graeme Pollock* (Sportsman Enterprises)
Danie Craven se top-Springbokke by *Hennie Gerber* (Tafelberg)
The South African Sporting Biography and Who's Who (Donaldsons)
The Story of Irish Rugby by *Edmund van Esbeck* (Stanley Paul)
The History of South African Rugby by *Ivor Difford* (The Speciality Press)
The Lions by *Wallace Reyburn* (Stanley Paul)
Lions Rampant by *Vivian Jenkins* (Cassell)
Fields of Praise by *David Smith & Gareth Williams* (University of Wales Press)
Ringside View by *A C Parker* (Howard Timmins)
The Springboks Talk by *Maxwell Price* (Howard Timmins)
The D B Draught Rugby Almanack of New Zealand
Green and Gold by *R K Stent* (Longmans)
The Rugby Football Internationals Roll of Honour by *E H D Sewell* (T C & E C Jack)
Rugby in South Africa (Johnston & Neville)
The History of the Laws of the Game by *Admiral Sir Percy Royds*
Die Stryd om die Curriebeker by *J D Roux* (J D R Publikasies)
My Recollections and Reminiscences by *W A Millar* (Juta)
Caught by the Springboks by *Jack Cheetham* (Howard Timmins)
Pillar to Post by *Stewart Ramsay, Dick Stent, Peter Atkins* (Don Nelson)
The South African Racehorse – May, 1987: Sea Cottage – the end of an era
Springbok Annals by *Danie Craven* (Mimosa)
South Africa's Greatest Springboks by *John E Sacks (Sporting Publications)*
Lord's by *John Marshall*
The All Blacks on Trek Again by *Winston McCarthy* (Sporting Publications)
The Olympic Games, edited by *Lord Killanin* & *John Rodda* (Macdonald & James)
The Guiness Book of Olympic Records edited by *Norris McWhirter* & *Sam Greenberg* (Penguin)
The Olympics 1896-1972 by *Ross McWhirter* (Scott International)
Playfair Olympics 1984 Los Angeles (Queen Anne Press)
Rothman's Rugby Yearbook (Queen Anne Press)

A

B

C

219

220

L

222

V

van den Bergh, Mauritz   49, 53
van der Merwe, Bertus   137
van der Merwe, Fiks   74
van der Merwe, Flippie   204
van der Merwe, Peter   144, 167-171, 173, 174, 190
van der Merwe, Stompie   155-157, 159
van der Ryst, Frans   107
van der Schyff, Jack   73-77, 132
van der Vyver, Fonnie   47, 49
van der Walt, Jumbo   159
van Jaarsveld, Hoppy   74
van Niekerk, Otto   74
van Reenen, George   49
van Ryneveld, Clive   108
van Schoor, Ryk   73, 102, 104, 107
van Tonder, André   155, 157, 159
van Veen, Hans   211
van Vollenhoven, Tom   133, 134, 135, 137
van Wyk, Basie   99, 101, 103, 104, 107
van Wyk, Rooies   155, 159
van Zijl, Fanie   212
Veivers, Tom   152
Verity, Hedley   39, 40, 42, 45
Verwey, Jock   160
Verwey, Bobby   160
Verwoerd H F   144, 198
Viljoen, Ken   39, 109, 116, 126, 130, 144, 152
Villet, John   207, 208
Vincent, Cyril   40
Visser, de Villiers   199
Viviers, Basie   107
Vogler, Ernie   11, 12, 15, 17-19, 21
Vorster, B J   144, 198, 210

W

Wade, Herbie   40-44
Wahl, Ballie   74, 76, 77

Waite, John   112, 115-117, 122, 125, 129, 144, 145, 147, 148, 167
Waller, Philip   30
Walter, Kenny   145
Walters, Doug   194, 195
Ward, Charles   64
Ward, R H   57
Warner, Sir Pelham   9-12, 14-20
Watkins, John   111-113, 116, 117, 121, 123-127
Watt, Howard   47, 49, 56
Webster, Jimmy   85
Wemyss, Jock   101
Wessels, Piet   99, 107
Westberg, J   37
White, Gordon   11, 13-15, 18-20
White, Jimmy   49, 50, 56
Whitington, Dick   147
Williams, Avril   208
Williams, D O   49, 50, 53, 55, 56
Williams, John   30
Williams, R H   137
Williams, W O G   137
Wilson, Charles   30
Wilson, Lionel   157, 159
Wilson, Robert   100
Wilson, Stu   200
Winslow, Charlie   66
Wintle, Bo   74
Wolmarans, Gert   143
Woodfull, W M   39
Woolley, Frank   171
Wright, Ron   111
Wyatt, R E S   39, 41, 43, 44
Wyatt, Wade   41
Wynard, E G   14, 17-19

Y

Yamasani   32

Z

Zeller, Bill   107